Housing Projects
Mansions and Schools
An Educator's Odyssey

Housing Projects
Mansions and Schools
An Educator's Odyssey

BY ROGER PROSISE

Chatter House Press
Indianapolis, Indiana

To: Wayne
Hope you like it
Roger Prosise

Housing Projects, Mansions, and Schools:
An Educator's Odyssey

Copyright© 2017 by Roger Prosise

Cover design by Kelsey Dunning

For information:

Chatter House Press
7915 S Emerson Ave, Ste B303
Indianapolis, IN 46237

chatterhousepress.com

ISBN: 978-1-937793-41-8
Library of Congress Control Number: 2017943408

Dedication

To my mother, Lucille Kojima Prosise,
who through sacrifice, love and hardwork,
enabled her kids to escape poverty.

Acknowledgements

I'll begin by thanking God for giving me a life filled with extraordinary experiences from being born and raised in Cabrini-Green in Chicago, the worst public housing project in the country, to becoming the superintendent of Bannockburn School, a school in one of the wealthiest communities in the country. The publication of this book is an answer to prayer.

I want to acknowledge and thank my mother, the backbone of my family when I was growing up. I also want to thank my wife Ellen for her support. Of my nine siblings, Aiko, Ellyn, Robert, Bill, Phyllis, Donna, Pat, Annette, and Linda, I want to give a special shout-out to my sisters Annette, Aiko, and Ellyn, for providing some background information on my mother and father.

My background is as an educator. And though I had some success with writing as an educator, I learned how to write this book by attending noncredit writing courses at the University of Iowa and the University of Chicago. From the University of Iowa, I want to thank Mary Allen for being my teacher and coach, and from the University of Chicago, instructor Kevin Davis.

I also want to thank and acknowledge my friends Antonio Gonzalez and Dr. Gerald Gutek for encouraging me to write this book, and Gerry Gutek for his advisement.

TABLE OF CONTENTS

PART I - CABRINI-GREEN

CHAPTER 1 5
CHAPTER 2 12
CHAPTER 3 18
CHAPTER 4 24
CHAPTER 5 33
CHAPTER 6 40
CHAPTER 7 43
CHAPTER 8 47
CHAPTER 9 55

PART II - LAKE VIEW

CHAPTER 10 61
CHAPTER 11 67
CHAPTER 12 70
CHAPTER 13 76

PART III - MANSIONS AND SCHOOLS

CHAPTER 14 85
CHAPTER 15 89
CHAPTER 16 93
CHAPTER 17 97
CHAPTER 18 102
CHAPTER 19 106
CHAPTER 20 110
CHAPTER 21 117
CHAPTER 22 130
CHAPTER 23 138

Prologue

I pull into the McDonald's parking lot and get out of my car. When I get through the door I see Juanita and Jeffrey, wife and son of Michael Jordan, sitting at a table in the corner. Juanita's wearing blue jeans and a beige top. Jeffrey's got on green shorts and a blue t- shirt. He's five years old and he sits there hunched over, stuffing fries into his mouth. It's the last week in August and school hasn't started yet. Next week Jeffrey will be entering kindergarten at Bannockburn School and I'll be starting my new job as superintendent there. Bannockburn, one hour north of Chicago, is one of the wealthiest villages in the country. I've met Juanita once before, in July when she stopped by the school to meet me because she'd heard there was going to be a new superintendent. She waves at me now and I venture over and say, "Hi, Juanita and Jeffrey."

It seems strange to be running into Juanita at McDonald's. I'm sure she's here because Jeffrey wanted a Happy Meal or something, but still, I wouldn't expect to find her here. But then, maybe she wouldn't expect to find me here either.

"Are you looking forward to school?" I ask them both.

"Jeffrey's excited," she says. "I heard Mrs. Hamilton is great." Jeffrey looks up from his fries and nods.

"I think you'll love it," I tell Jeffrey.

"Have you met Michael yet?" Juanita asks.

"No, I haven't."

"He's going to drop Jeffrey off at school next week. Introduce yourself. I'm going to tell him to look for you."

"Great. I will. Thanks. Enjoy your lunch."

I walk over to the counter and place my order. As I eat my Big Mac and drink my Coke at a small table by the windows I realize I haven't been thinking at all about the fact that Michael Jordan's son goes to my new school. I've focused all my energy on how to do a good job as a superintendent in this wealthy community. My background is anything but wealthy. I was a poor kid but no one else here at Bannockburn knows that, and I want to keep it that way. If you were never poor, you might not understand. So far in my career as an educator I've worked in inner-city or middle-class schools and I haven't really adjusted yet to being here. The school board that hired me, the few parents and teachers I've met have all welcomed me warmly to Bannockburn. Still, I feel uneasy because my personal background isn't a match for Bannockburn.

I'm a huge basketball fan and I suddenly feel thrilled at the idea of meeting Michael Jordan. And then, as I sit here in a patch of sunlight eating my fries, I think about how far I've come—from growing up in Cabrini-Green, a public housing project that would see the worst racial rioting in the country a few months after my family moved out— how I've taught in high-poverty schools and middle-class white schools where black kids were bussed in, and how I've ended up here, in this town where the median price of houses is close to a million dollars and where celebrities live and send their kids to my school.

Part I
Cabrini-Green

Chapter 1

Twelve Hours

Mike and I were standing in front of the Music Box theater on Southport Street in Chicago, looking at posters of the Dirty Dozen. The Music Box was one block away from my new apartment and Mike was my first friend in my new neighborhood. A ticket cost fifty cents.

"Want to go next week?" Mike asked.

At eight o'clock this morning my family and I still lived in Cabrini-Green, and now, at eight o'clock at night, I lived in Lake View, a peaceful middle-class neighborhood where mostly Irish and German people lived. I was hapa—half-white, half-Asian— and my skin color would fit in a lot better here. We moved after the guy who painted our townhouse—every five years the Chicago Housing Authority had its section VIII housing touched up—told my mother there was a vacancy in a two-flat apartment building he owned in a nicer neighborhood. Over coffee my mother worked out a plan with him to transfer our section VIII (subsidized housing) agreement to his apartment building in Lake View. Before we moved she warned my father that if he didn't stop drinking he would be left behind.

At nine o'clock this morning—the last Saturday in September 1967, the beginning of my eighth grade year—a deacon from our church had driven a big U-haul truck here in Cabrini with all our stuff in it. I sat in the front seat next to the deacon, Mr. Hirata. My oldest sister, Aiko, was following in her car, my father sitting in the front seat next to her and my mother in the back. Eddie—we always called my father Eddie—couldn't get into the backseat because he had arthritis. He couldn't help unload the truck when we got to our new house either, so he watched and supervised while my brothers, sisters, and I unloaded it and my mother started emptying the boxes in the kitchen.

While we were unloading the truck, Mike, a freckle-faced kid with a blond crewcut and glasses, came out of the two-story red-brick building and offered to help, but I told him we had plenty of help—I've got nine brothers and sisters and they were all here. My oldest sister Aiko was ten years older than me and my youngest sister Linda was seven years younger. There were seven girls and three boys. My sister Aiko had driven my older brothers and my sisters over earlier when the deacon brought other truckloads. Mike told me he was in eighth grade and lived on the first floor and would come back later and show me around the neighborhood.

Now in front of the Music Box, I looked at Mike, grinned and said, "I'd love to go see The Dirty Dozen. I like movies." We made plans to go to the movie next Saturday night at eight. In my old neighborhood I always had to take a bus to get to a movie, and I never went to the show with friends. Instead I went with my mother on my day off, and I always paid for my mother's ticket. I'd started making money two summers ago working on a polo ranch about forty-five minutes from where we lived. I was saving most of that money for the new car I wanted to buy when I was old enough to drive. I loved my mother and it made me happy to take her to the movies on Monday, her day off from her job cleaning houses and my day off at the polo ranch during the summer. My two older brothers did the same thing.

Mike and I walked up and down Southport looking in store windows. It was my first night in this neighborhood but Mike had lived here for most of his life and he kept up a running commentary about everything as we walked. The street lights lit up the dark night. We both liked the blue tanker, a World War II bomber-type coat, in the window of the Southport Department Store. I knew my parents would never be able to buy it for me and I didn't want to spend the money myself. People were standing and sitting on the steps of two- and three-story brick apartment buildings. Cars were everywhere, parked on the street and passing us as we walked on the sidewalk inhaling fumes. There were hardly any cars in my old neighborhood, either parked or being driven. I was comfortable in my t-shirt and blue jeans. It was the end of September and it had been cool all day long and now in the evening it was a bit cooler.

I looked up at the stars in the sky thinking I was thirteen years old and my real life was just beginning. I had never walked around at night in Cabrini. There were no stores or movie theaters there. Instead there was street after street of rowhouses -- we lived in one of them, at 842 North Cleveland -- and beyond the rowhouses were the high-rise housing projects. The streets in Cabrini were empty at night. The few times I ventured out it was to buy a newspaper, tomorrow's Sun Times, for my father, who didn't work and liked to have the newspaper to read to pass the time. I always walked straight to the newspaper stand in the lobby of the Montgomery Ward catalog division near the Chicago River and straight back home. I was always aware of my skin color and wanted to avoid any kind of trouble.

But now, in Lake View, I could walk around freely without having to worry about sticking out because of the color of my skin. From Southport we walked to Clark Street. Mike said his dad was a bus driver and we might see him driving the Clark Street bus. On Clark Street a bus drove past us and the driver beeped and waved.

"Hey," Mike yelled, waving back. "That's my dad," he told me.

We sauntered down Clark Street past a bar and a laundromat and went into a corner drug store. We stood in front of a wall of magazines, looking at Sports Illustrated and Life, and then Mike bought a pack of gum and asked me if I wanted anything. I shook my head.

"Let's head back," Mike said. "Maybe some of the other guys will be outside on Janssen." Janssen was my new street. Mike lived downstairs from my new apartment, with his mother and father and older sister Lila who was the same age as my sister Donna, one year older than Mike and me. Donna would be a freshman at Lake View High School on Monday.

"Like who?" I asked.

"Eddie and Johnny Siebert live across the street from us." I thought it was interesting that there was a kid living here named Eddie. Eddie was my father's name—my brothers and sisters and I all called him that; he said it made him feel younger than being called Dad. "Eddie and Johnny are both in eighth grade like us," Mike told me. "Johnny's a year older. He was held back a year in school. They might be outside. Gibby Monroe lives across the street too. He's in seventh. I play football in the street with those guys a lot. Do you like football?

"Yeah. It's my favorite sport."

"Cool. Where'd you live before?"

"Cabrini-Green."

"No way. Isn't Cabrini all black?"

"When we moved we were pretty much the only white family there. But, let's talk about Blaine because I'm starting there on Monday. I can tell you about Cabrini another time."

My first day at my new school was two days away, on Monday. I'd spent my first month of eighth grade at Cooley Junior High School in Cabrini. I was nervous and excited to be transferring to Blaine. I'd gone to school in Cabrini my whole life. Would I be accepted and make new friends here? It was getting a little scary at Cooley -- some of the high school kids who didn't want me in their neighborhood because of the color of my skin, had started harassing me in seventh grade and were doing it more often now that I was an eighth grader.

"Do you know whose room you'll be in?" Mike asked me.

"Nope. Guess I'll find out on Monday."

"Just so you know, all eighth graders have a science test on Monday. You might not have to take it since you're new but who knows; you can borrow my notes if you want to."

I hated science. It was my least favorite subject. "Thanks," I said "I will."

It was getting dark so we walked down Grace Street back to Janssen. People were still sitting outside with their kids on their porches chatting with neighbors. Back at Janssen, in front of my new home, I met a few of the other guys who lived on our block.

Eddie, Johnny, and Gibby lived across the street from Mike and me. That night we hung out on Janssen Street and talked under the streetlights. Johnny and Gibby sat on the hoods of cars parked on the street. Eddie, Mike, and I stood around with our hands in our pockets, talking and enjoying the cool night air.

"I know you just moved in, but how do you like it so far? Where'd you live before?" asked Gibby.

" I think I'm going to like it here. I was in Cabrini-Green before," I said.

"Isn't Cabrini all black? How'd you survive?" Gibby said. He jumped down off the car and paced back and forth in the empty street. Johnny jumped from his perch on the hood. He gave me a look of disbelief too and so did Eddie.

"Pretty much," I said. "It wasn't too bad. I had friends and I got picked on a little but not that much." Six months after we moved out of there, some of the worst rioting in the country over the assassination of Dr. Martin Luther King Jr. occurred in Cabrini-Green. But that hadn't happened yet on this night.

"You should like it here," said Gibby. "Wait til you see Miss. Anderson the PE teacher." He started telling me about her nice body. In the middle of the description of her muscular thighs, a kid named Harold Joseph, a pale skin kid with red combed back hair and freckles, came by on his bike with a few of his friends. The talking ended and the air became tense. Gibby's eyes grew wide and he stepped away from us. Harold got off his bike and for no apparent reason pushed Johnny. He didn't push back so Harold pushed Johnny more. I couldn't believe what was happening. No way this dorky kid is pushing us around, I thought. Even though I just met Johnny, I started walking toward Harold, thinking I'm not taking this. I didn't let kids push me around in Cabrini and it wasn't going to start now. You had to fight to survive in Cabrini.

"Who's the new kid?" Harold said and stepped toward me. "You want some too?"

I stomped my foot hard and he jumped. He started swinging at me and missing. I slapped him in the face a few times, thinking this kid is a punk. He quit fighting, got on his bike, and left with his friends. My new friends were relieved and surprised. We laughed and joked about it.

"I'm glad you're from Cabrini," Gibby said.

"You know Harold's older brother is in the MG's," Eddie said.

"What's the MG's?" I asked.

"A neighborhood gang. They live over on Magnolia and Grace," Eddie answered.

I was surprised to hear about gangs being here. There were gangs in Cabrini. They left me alone but they tried to recruit my friends, who ran away from them.

"He'll be too embarrassed to say anything," said Gibby.

I felt glad I stood up to Harold. I had a few fights in Cabrini and this was nothing. It felt good and got me instant cred.

It was getting late and we decided to go home.

"Tell me what you think of Miss Anderson after you see her on Monday," yelled Gibby as he crossed the street on his way to his apartment building.

"I will," I yelled. I stopped at Mike's and picked up his notes. "I'll get these back to you tomorrow, thanks," I said. "Don't forget man, I want to hear about Cabrini."

When I got upstairs I helped my mother and sisters unpack the few remaining boxes.

"You were gone for a long time. What did you do?" my mom said as she washed the dishes that had been wrapped in newspaper.

"I was just walking around with Mike and hanging out with a few other guys out in front," I said.

"It didn't take long for you to make some friends."

"I know. I like our new house," I said thinking my future looks nothing like my past. In the projects there were no stores or a movie theater and I never walked around at night.

Before I went to bed, I sat on the living room floor and read Mike's science notes over and over. I memorized the steps of the scientific method. I wanted to do well on the test. I'd done well in school before the move.

I went down the hall to my room, put on my pajamas, and climbed up onto my bunk, and crawled under the covers. Just like in Cabrini I shared a bedroom with my two older brothers. My mother and five of my sisters slept in the other three bedrooms. My two oldest sisters were out of the house. One was away at college and one had her own apartment. There was a triple bunk bed in this room, the room I shared with my older brothers, Robert and Bill. I slept on top. It wasn't as bad as it sounds -- we weren't there that much, we used the room only to sleep and dress in. My father was in the enclosed porch behind my bedroom. He always slept alone. He drank in Cabrini and I would learn later that he didn't when we moved to Lake View.

I closed my eyes, but instead of going to sleep right away I thought about Cabrini-Green and what I should tell Mike. He was awfully curious.

Chapter 2

Cabrini-Green

Today, as I write this, it's forty-eight years after the day I sat outside on my new porch steps and told Mike about Cabrini-Green. Cabrini-Green is now known as River North, an up-and-coming Chicago neighborhood. Between 2000 to 2005, total sales of residential properties in the River North area neared $1 billion. Since the mid-1990s, Chicago has torn down eighty-two public high rises throughout the city, and in March 2011 the last of the twenty-four towers in Cabrini came down. Cabrini has come to embody a nightmare vision of public housing. The apartments in the old buildings were subsidized by the federal government, but a condo in the new high rises sells for $500,000.

Even before its current gentrification, the neighborhood went through many changes. It started out as Swede Town—many Swedish immigrants came to Chicago in the 1870s, and most of them lived in Swede Town—and then in the early twentieth century became known as Little Hell or Little Sicily, after many Italian immigrants moved in. Little Hell was notorious for its inhabitants' poverty and its dilapidated buildings. The Chicago Housing Authority demolished it and built nine blocks of brick rowhouses. The rowhouses were created in 1942 for World War II workers to live in, and were named after Mother Frances Cabrini, an Italian nun who was the first naturalized U.S. citizen to be canonized by the Catholic church.

Demographics in Chicago¹ continued changing. At one point in the 1940s 3,000 African Americans stepped off busses and trains from the South every week to start new lives in Chicago. In response, the Chicago Housing Authority decided to provide decent housing to low-income families, and in 1958 fifteen red-brick high rises, called Cabrini Extension, went up half a mile away from the Frances Cabrini rowhouses. In 1962 the CHA built three more white-stone high rises containing 1,096 more units, called the William Green Homes, and the neighborhood became known as Cabrini-Green.

Back in the 1940s, when the rowhouses were first built, white, black, Hispanic, and Asian families all lived in the neighborhood, but over the years most families that could afford to move out of Cabrini did, and by the early-1960s, when I was growing up there, the population was 99 percent African-American. Although we were practically the only white family still living there then, I learned how to survive mostly by minding my own business and staying out of trouble. Six months after we moved out of Cabrini-Green, some of the worst rioting in the country over the assassination of Dr. Martin Luther King, Jr., occurred there. Buildings and cars were set on fire and stores were looted. Cabrini-Green was on the national news and became thought of as the worst public housing project in the nation.

Based on what I've read in the years since, gangs and drug sales ran rampant in Cabrini, but I didn't see much evidence of that when I lived there. I do remember seeing guys walking around dressed in fancy dress pants and fedora hats but I didn't have any idea what that was about—where they got the money to buy that kind of clothes. All I thought was that they were cool, although I know now from my older brother that they were drug dealers. I also knew then, and I still know it, that parents in Cabrini valued education and participated in school functions like parent-teacher conferences. Now, from my current vantage point as someone who has worked as a teacher and an educator for thirty-three years, I see that the education offered in Cabrini-Green, at least when I was living there, was good. The teachers I had when I went to grammar school there were as good as any I had anywhere. The teachers at Jenner always gave work that sparked my interest and we rarely had free time.

In 1965, when I was in sixth grade at Jenner, my teacher, Ms. Gunther, a white woman and longtime educator, who was strict but also inspired me to try my best, resigned mid-year. At the end of her last day, she gave us all a letter to bring home to our parents explaining that she was leaving. She didn't say why, but now, I suspect, from my vantage point as a retired school superintendent, that she didn't agree with the new principal, Miss Chuchett's, management style. When I arrived at school the following Monday, I saw about fifteen parents marching back and forth in front of the school with picket signs demanding the principal's resignation; they were also chanting, "Ms. Chuchutt must go." When I got to class I noticed that about half the seats were empty in my classroom— the parents in front of the school must've also kept their kids home. All those parents were black. My parents didn't picket, my mother had to work and my father rarely left the house, but they supported Mrs. Gunther too. My family watched the news that night. There they were, all those African-American parents supporting a white teacher. This says to me that education transcended race in Cabrini-Green.

Mrs. Gunther never came back and the new principal didn't resign. Mr. Kasey was my new teacher and after two days things went back to normal.

There may have been other problems in Cabrini that I wasn't aware of as a kid, or that developed after we moved. When I was a college student at University of Illinois/Chicago in the early 1970s one of the students in my history class was a Chicago police officer, and when I told him I grew up in Cabrini, he said that the police had stopped responding to emergency calls from Cabrini because when they did people threw bottles at them from the high rises -- he seemed to think the calls were just an excuse to get them there. Recently I read about Cabrini in a book called High Rise Stories: Voices From Chicago Public Housing. That book said that after Martin Luther King, Jr., was assassinated in 1968, snipers began shooting indiscriminately from upper stories in the high rises in Cabrini-Green, a practice that continued sporadically for decades. And someone I met not long ago told me one of his friends, a Chicago police officer, was shot and killed in the 1970s when he was on duty in Cabrini-Green.

The high rises always scared me when we lived in Cabrini. They were the unknown, especially when I was alone. Looking back now as an adult, I'm thankful that we moved out of the neighborhood when we did. I wonder what would have happened to me and family, as part of the one percent of nonblack people there, during the rioting.

Sitting out on the stoop on the second day of my new home at 3752 North Janssen, I told my new friend Mike that we hardly ever saw cars in Cabrini-Green. Any time we went somewhere we either walked or took the bus or someone picked us up. We kids played in the street all the time and got out of the way whenever a car came along.

My family shopped at an A&P grocery store that was a mile away from our house, on Larrabee Street, a busy street beyond the northern part of the projects in Cabrini. My mother walked the eight blocks there once a week on Saturday, pulling a gray metal-frame shopping cart, and bought four bags of groceries. My mother was a tiny Japanese-American woman, barely five feet tall, who worked full time and raised ten kids. She was the backbone of our family and my brothers and sisters and I all loved and admired her, even when she yelled at us for teasing my younger sister or ignoring her when she stood on the front step and called out that dinner was ready and we should come home.

She cleaned houses five days a week to support us and on her day off she vacuumed and dusted the living room—sweeping the kitchen floor was one of my chores and my sisters cleaned the bathrooms—and then she did the laundry for all twelve of us, washing it in an old wringer washing machine in our utility room and hanging it out to dry on the clothesline in the backyard or, in the winter, draping it around the house. Then she went to the grocery store. I or one of my brothers or sisters usually went with her to help and got a treat like a candy bar or ice cream cone for a reward.

There was only one place to buy candy in the rowhouses that I knew of -- Mr. Tootsie's house, a rowhouse one block away from ours. Mr. Tootsie was a small soft spoken old man with coffee-colored skin and gray hair. He sold penny candy and small toys out of his home; he'd set up a portable glass case at the top of the stairs on the second floor. I bought candy from Mr. Tootsie if I got my twenty-five cents allowance at the end of the week for doing my chores. I always did my chores but I didn't get my allowance when my father got drunk. My favorite candy was nut chews. I bought a small bag of marbles for a nickle from Mr. Tootsie at the beginning of the summer vacation and played marbles all summer with my friends in the dirt in my front yard.

I think of life in Cabrini in terms of things we didn't have. Discretionary income was foreign to us. Sammy's hot dog stand was the only restaurant in Cabrini-Green. Almost none of us had cars, and only one family I knew went on vacation, the family with the car. There was no playground equipment for kids. We played simple games like marbles, football, and ledge ball. The girls played hopscotch and jumped rope. Double-dutch was popular. The boys slap-boxed for fun, like boxing with open hands -- a lot.

I played outside almost all the time when I lived in Cabrini-Green. I played football and red rover with my friends in the street and in the backyards. During the school year I had to finish my homework before I went outside to play. I bought a bike from a friend with a ten-dollar bill I found on the street and after that I rode my bike with other kids and we had bike races around the block.

Mike looked at me after I told him all that, sitting on the stoop in my new neighborhood. "Wow, man!" he said as if he could hardly believe it. "No stores or restaurants?" There was a movie theater, a department store, a drugstore, and a small grocery store, Nick's, all within a block of my new home.

We went down to the basement of our building, where our bikes were stored. Mike found his, a blue Schwinn, and I found mine, the red twenty-inch boy's bike that I'd bought from a kid in Cabrini, where I'd leaned it against the basement wall yesterday. We carried the bikes upstairs to the sidewalk, jumped on, and rode around my new neighborhood.

"Let's go to the next block. Phyllis Dipetro lives on that block. She's in my homeroom," Mike yelled. So we rode past the church on the corner, past the brick apartment buildings and the trees and the streetlights. And peddling my bike down the street in the cool evening air, without worrying about sticking out or having to be on guard, I felt something light and happy inside me, almost as if I was flying instead of riding.

Chapter 3

Fitting In

Even though my skin color was different from almost everybody else's in Cabrini I still had plenty of friends. Almost all of the white families had moved out over the years so all of my friends were black. When a family could afford to move out of Cabrini they did.

One of my best friends in grammar school and during the first year of junior high was Michael Walker. He was an inch taller than I was and had walnut-brown skin. He brought comic books from home and shared them with me when it was raining and we had to stay in during recess. When it was nice and we went outside for recess, he and I stuck together.

Michael got good grades and was one of the smartest kids in school. He always raised his hand when the teacher asked questions. He didn't run very fast and he wasn't very strong, but he always played the games everybody played, like red rover. Michael never started a fight but he didn't back down either. He was witty and always had a come-back if someone messed with him. He lived in a high rise and liked Linda Thurmond who was in our home room in both grammar school and junior high and lived in the high rise building next to his so sometimes he followed her home. She was a tall girl with a mean temper. She didn't like Michael, but that didn't phase him one bit.

We didn't have a playground with swings at Jenner. So instead of swinging on swings or kicking balls we fought for fun during recess. In fourth grade it was my homeroom against the room next door day after day for about two weeks. Michael and I and most of the rest of the boys in Mrs. Gray's class charged into the boys from the other room, who were huddling in wait by the corner of the building. When we ran at them they flailed their arms and fists for protection and swung at us while we swung at them. No one ever got hurt. My friend Milton didn't join us because he didn't want to get into trouble—Milton never did anything he wasn't supposed to do—but he got into trouble just like the rest of us when Mrs. Gray found out what we were doing and made us all stay in from recess for a week. After that we stopped battling the other homeroom and it wasn't until we were in seventh grade that we found other ways to fight for fun.

Milton lived in a rowhouse across the backyard from ours so he was both a neighborhood friend and a school friend. Milton was in fourth grade with me and everyone liked him, including the teacher. I was a little jealous of him. He was my height and had long muscular arms and big eyes and a big smile with even teeth. Whenever we were picking sides for teams he was always picked before me which made me more jealous. His whole family went to church on Sunday, not just the kids like in my family. Unlike my father, his father had a car and a job, working at a printing company. Milton went with his parents and brother and sisters on a family vacation to Arkansas every summer for a week. Milton's grandparents and aunts and uncles and cousins still lived in Arkansas and Milton had moved to Chicago from there. I wondered what that was like, getting in a car and driving to a different state. I didn't know it at the time, but Milton's family's move was part of the Second Great Migration from the South, which started in 1940 and resulted in the Cabrini-Green high rises being built in the 1950s.

Sometimes Milton and I and some other kids played baseball with my older brothers in an open field a block from our house. I couldn't hit or catch ground balls but Milton caught fly balls and got on base when it was his turn to bat. He played right field and I played second base. Once the first baseman threw me the ball when a runner on first tried to steal and I put up my glove and the ball hit me in the eye. My eye started to swell. I got scared and felt embarrassed. My older brother Billy put his hand on my head, looked at my eye and told me to go home. I walked home feeling dejected. When I got home I went straight to my mom.

"What happened?" she asked looking at my eye.

"I got hit with the ball,"

"I'm sorry. Come here." She hugged me and put the bag of ice on my eye.

I missed playing baseball that day but loved being with my mom.

Milton's family moved out of Cabrini when we were at the end of sixth grade so Milton didn't go to Cooley and I never saw him again. I met Lorenzo at Cooley and we became best friends. Lorenzo was five-foot-nine and had dark brown skin and a big friendly smile. He was muscular but not bulky and was always laughing about something. We both liked sports and girls. Football was our favorite sport. The only time we played sports was during gym—we didn't have recess at Cooley. At Cooley we slap-boxed for fun. Slap boxing is like boxing except with an open hand. My seventh grade teacher had no control of the class and every afternoon three or four boys would take turns going into the hall to slap box. My friend Lorenzo beat everyone. He had quick hands and always got the best of me, but I did pretty well when I boxed with all the other guys. Lorenzo lived in the white stone high rises like Philip, my friend in sixth grade who didn't go to Cooley.

Philip moved to Cabrini during the summer before sixth grade so he was a new kid at Jenner when we started school that fall. I'd gone to school there since kindergarten and knew the ropes and I befriended him on his first day. He had light brown skin and freckles and he smiled all the time. In November the school started offering Social Center two hours after school once a week, where kids could hang around in the school basement playing ping pong and bumper pool. The first time I went I felt a little out of place; I was a white kid there among hundreds of unfamiliar black faces instead of a white kid among twenty-five familiar black faces like I was in class. Phillip stayed with me the whole time; we played ping pong together, which I knew how to play, and then bumper pool, which I wasn't very good at because I had never played it before.

A couple of weeks after that Phillip invited me to come over to his house after school. I never went to anybody's house in Cabrini. The kids I knew outside of school were from my neighborhood and we knew each other because we all played together in the street. Even though I had never been inside any of my friends' houses and I didn't have permission from my parents, I decided to go to Phillip's when he invited me. He lived in one of the white stone high rises on Division Street.

When we crossed Larabee Street we saw a group of seven high school boys dressed in jeans and baggy shirts, hanging around the entrance of the high rise. They stared at me as we approached the building and I felt uneasy and out of place. "He's cool," Philip told them. "A friend from school." They looked away and nodded. One flicked his cigarette onto the sidewalk and said, "Alright, Phillip."

We walked into the building and down the hall to the elevator. The halls smelled of urine and the walls were spray-painted with swear words and gang signs. We took the elevator to the tenth floor. I followed Philip down the hall and he opened the door to his apartment with a key. Once we were inside I stayed by the door while Phillip stepped into the kitchen where his mother, father, and sister were standing by the table. Before Phillip could say anything his father said, loud enough for everyone to hear, "Get that white boy out of my house."

I was embarrassed and a little angry and could feel my face getting red. No adult had ever treated me like an intruder in their house or in the neighborhood because of my skin color before, and it shocked me to hear it now from Phillip's father. It wasn't my decision to live in Cabrini, I thought.

Philip turned around and looked at me. I could see in his face that he felt even more embarrassed than I did. "Sorry, man. I wasn't expecting that. We better go."

"It's alright. It's not your fault," I said.

Phillip took the elevator down with me and walked me out to Division Street. I crossed the street and headed down Cleveland Street.

As I walked home alone on that late Friday afternoon, a white face among hundreds of unfamiliar black faces, I felt like an outsider, like a stranger here. I would never fit in here, I realized, even though I had always tried to, listening to the radio station my friends all listened to, WVON, which played music by James Brown and the Temptations and Smokey Robinson and the Miracles, thinking one of the girls at school, Sherry, liked me and it didn't matter that I was white. Before this moment I hadn't really understood something that I understood now, that Phillip's father's words had made me understand: Race did matter.

As much as I had tried, I didn't fit in, my skin color was different than that of almost everybody. Not fitting in was hard but I didn't think about it much until that time in Philip's hallway. Cabrini-Green was a world unto itself and my view of the world was limited. I had no clue that black people struggled to fit in most communities outside of Cabrini-Green.

Of course now I know differently. As an adult I know that police treat black men like second class citizens. Today as I write this there appears to be an epidemic of police shooting young black men. Schools filled with black students are inferior and jails are filled with black men. Several years ago when I was tutoring a senior at Holy Trinity High School on the north side of the city, he told me that when he was a freshman, his counselor told him and three of his friends that the odds were only one of them would graduate. And, he told me, as we sat there across from each other at a Starbucks with his English paper between us, the prophecy came true: One of his three friends had been killed in a shooting and the other two were in jail. And, he was the only one graduating from high school and thanks to the Posse Foundation was on his way to Oberlin College on a four year scholarship.

But when I was growing up in Cabrini-Green, I didn't think much about racism. I had my first taste of it in Philip's apartment and unlike most white people, I was on the receiving end of it. When I got to Lake View I still didn't know much about racism, I just knew that I fit in better. And when I look back on my years in Cabrini, I wonder what would have happened to me if I didn't have friends. I don't think about black or white friends. I think about friends.

If not for my friends in Cabrini, life would have been unbearable. Lorenzo stood up for me and saved me from getting beat up from the high school kids at Cooley. Philip played ping pong and pool with me at the after school social center. After school I played outside everyday with my neighborhood friends, Milton, Karl, Lamont and Glen. And when I walked a mile to return a book to my old sixth grade teacher, my neighborhood friends went with me. I'm horrified to think that boys like my friends are being shot or sent to jail, made to feel different and inferior. I'm not glad I had to live in Cabrini-Green, but I'm glad for my friends there and for the chance to learn something about the world and myself.

Chapter 4

Backbone

I walked to the end of the block and turned right. I was heading to the incinerator to throw out the garbage. The incinerator was at the end of the rowhouses one block over from the row we lived in, and as I crossed the street I stayed on the look-out for Anthony. Anthony was nine like me but he was a little bigger than I was and he was a bully. I tried to avoid him whenever I took the garbage out—one of my chores was to take the garbage out every day. When I went to the incinerator last week he picked a fight and gave me a bloody lip. I hadn't seen him again and today when I made it to the incinerator and threw my garbage away I thought I'd avoided him again. But then, as I started walking back home, I saw him coming along the street behind me. He saw me and walked fast to catch up to me. I couldn't get away without running and I was too proud to run.

"Where you think you're going?" he said, catching his breath.

"Home," I answered.

"What'd you say about my mother?" he said, trying to pick a fight.

"I didn't say anything about your mother."

He got in front of me and hit me in the face. "Don't talk about my mother," he said.

I swung and hit him in the side of the head. Then he hit me in the nose. I heard a crunch and my nose started bleeding. I turned and walked quickly toward home with blood streaming down my face. Anthony didn't follow me. I walked past some neighbors standing outside their houses. I knew they saw me but I didn't care. I went all the way home with my hands covering my face with blood running down it. When I got home, my mother took one look at me and got furious.

"Who did this to you?" she asked.

"Anthony," I said.

"Do you know where he lives?"

I nodded.

She took me by the arm and we rushed along the street to Anthony's house, a block away. My mother knocked and Anthony and his mom both came to the door. "Look what your son did to my boy," my mother said through the screen door, pointing at me.

Anthony's mother asked him if that was true and he said yes but I started the fight which I didn't. I looked at my mother and saw she didn't believe I had started the fight. Anthony's mother told him to stay away from me. My nose was still bleeding when my mother and I walked back home. The neighbors stared at us as though we were strangers, even though we'd lived a block away from them for over ten years. My mother took my hand and I glanced at her serious face. She looked back at me briefly, then stared straight ahead as we walked along. I always loved my mother, but in that moment I loved her even more.

My mother was Japanese-American. She was born in 1922 in Greeley, Colorado. Her parents had a farm with chickens, cows and apple trees. The farm was confiscated by the U.S. government sometime after Pearl Harbor as part of the dispossession of Japanese Americans occurring at that time. Some historians believe that the seizure of farms belonging to Japanese Americans, who controlled much of the fruit and vegetable market in the west before the war, had more to do with eliminating economic competition and with the interests to get possession of the Japanese farms, than with any perceived threats from the Japanese Americans themselves.

My mother lived through a lot of deaths in her family. Her little brother died from diphtheria when she was five and her older sister died from the measles a year later. Two years later, when my mother was eight, her mother died of measles also. After her father lost his farm he decided to move back to Japan; on the way he stopped in southern California and left my mother there with friends, a Japanese-American family. The reasons he left my mother behind no longer survive in my family history, but I imagine he might have thought she'd have a chance for a better life in America, despite the war and the internment camps, than she would in Japan. My mother was a teenager when her father went back to Japan. When she was twenty years old she and her foster family were sent to Manzanar, one of ten internment camps that had been set up across the country.

They were called internment camps because if they were called concentration camps they would have been subject to international inspection under the Geneva Convention. Over 120,00 Japanese-Americans were relocated to the camps, two-thirds of whom were American citizens, usually after being given only days to gather their belongings. Ten thousand were sent to Manzanar. The camps ranged in severity from Manzanar, in southern California, where men sneaked out of camp at night to fish in a nearby lake, to Tule Lake in northern California, a prisoner-of-war camp where Japanese-American citizens suspected of being spies were sent. The men who sneaked out at night to fish were free and thought only about fishing, even if for a brief time. After eighteen months, men sneaked out and were gone for days fishing in the Sierra East mountains hours away from camp. The guards came to realize that these people imprisoned because of their race weren't the enemy, but in fact, were just like them, Americans.

Tule Lake, on the other hand, was a violent place where pro-Japan activists terrorized Japanese-Americans who were loyal to the United States. When the internees started protesting over the living conditions, the American Army was brought in to suppress them and protect the administration. Recently I met a man at an American Legion luncheon, Susumu Funai, who had been sent to Tule Lake as a kid. He and his family were transferred to Tule Lake from Heart Mountain, an "easier" internment camp in Wyoming, when the U.S. government found out that his father was a Buddhist priest and decided he was a spy. When I met him, Mr. Funai told me people were tortured at Tule Lake. He didn't say anything more about it and I didn't ask him, but I wondered if he was talking about his father. Research by Barbara Takei suggests that torture was used at Tule Lake. It was recognized as the only maximum-security center among the ten concentration camps.

After signing a loyalty oath, thousands of Japanese-American young men served in the U.S. military while their families were imprisoned in a camp. Japanese-Americans served in the Army's 442nd regiment and became the most decorated unit in the U.S. military. Thousands of Japanese-Americans fought and died for their country, the United States, while their families were imprisoned in a camp.

My mother was in Manazar for almost two years. Manzanar was the first internment camp and the most famous. She didn't talk about it much when I was growing up except to say it wasn't that bad, and maybe it wasn't that hard, compared to living on welfare in Cabrini-Green, cleaning houses five days a week, being married to an alcoholic, and raising ten kids. She did tell my younger sister Annette, when Annette was in her twenties, that Manzanar was hot and dusty and surrounded by barbed wire and guard towers. She tried to have as much fun there as she could, like any normal young person, but she and her friends couldn't go anywhere and had to stick to a strict routine. Although my mother always said she didn't hate being in the camp the way most of the people there hated it, I'm sure being confined in what was essentially a prison, because of her race, must've had an effect on her.

My mother left Manzanar to work as a maid for a woman from Kalamazoo named Mrs. Bardeen, in the early spring of 1944. The camp closed on November 1, 1945, two months after the war ended; the incarcerees were responsible for finding their own ways home. Nobody could get out before then unless they were sponsored by an American citizen, and Mrs. Bardeen sponsored my mother; her husband was a factory-owner, and I imagine he turned to Manzanar for cheap labor and that's how Mrs. Bardeen got connected with my mother. My mother was pregnant with my oldest sister Aiko when she left the camp for Michigan. She had Aiko in Kalamazoo and lived there for another year and a half. I'm pretty sure Mrs. Bardeen supported my mother throughout her pregnancy; they became friends and wrote letters and visited each other after my mother moved to Chicago to live with her cousin, my Uncle Tony, and his wife. In Chicago my mother got a job as a maid in the Edgewater Beach Hotel, a popular hotel at the time, and met my father, who was a waiter at the Edgewater. She thought he was funny and he was tall and debonaire and she wanted a father for her baby, so she married him.

In 1988, two Congressmen and a California senator wrote a bill that granted reparations to Japanese Americans who had been interned by the U.S. during the war. The language in the legislation said that government actions were based on "race prejudice, war hysteria, and a failure of political leadership." Ronald Reagan signed it into law, although a majority of Republicans voted against it. The act granted each internee $20,000. I remember when my mother got her check in the mail. She was sixty-two then and still lived in our old apartment in Lake View and worked in a doctor's office answering phones and doing clerical work. She used the money to pay bills and buy presents for all of us. She almost never spent money on herself.

In 1977 my older sister Aiko bought an apartment building with six apartments in Lake View on Byron, a few blocks away from our old apartment on Janssen, where we moved after our time in Cabrini. My mother and father and two of my sisters moved into a three-bedroom apartment on the second floor and six years later, my wife and I and my new baby daughter Lauren moved into a different apartment in the same building. My mother eventually moved into a smaller apartment across the hall in the same building and lived there for most of the rest of her life.

I remember a family dinner in my mother's apartment in 1993. By then my wife and I and our two kids—our second daughter Kristen was three by then, our third child, Kevin, hadn't been born yet—lived in a house in Morton Grove, a suburb fifteen minutes north of Chicago. I had been the principal of Hynes School in Morton Grove for two years and was looking for a different job. It was Sunday evening and the plates and forks were on the table in the dining room when we arrived. Sunday dinner was important to my mom. My mom was cooking in the kitchen wearing a flower-printed apron. We were having fried chicken with mashed potatoes and corn on the cob. My mother put the food on platters and my sisters Aiko, Ellyn, Annette and Phyllis, who lived in two separate apartments in the building—Aiko and Ellyn lived together and Phyllis and Annette lived together—brought the platters out to the table. I filled glasses with water at the kitchen sink and set them on the dining room table. The smell of fried chicken filled the air.

When we started eating I told everyone I was thinking of applying for a job in Urbana, Illinois, to be a middle school principal. I loved college towns and I liked being a principal so the move made a lot of sense to me. After my announcement I looked at my mom. Her eyes were filled with sadness and disappointment. "Don't move to Urbana," she said. "What's wrong with staying here? You have a good job."

"I don't know," I said. "Nothing's wrong with Hynes, but I want to live in a college town. We could come back and visit once a month."

"No, you won't," said my mom.

"I'll have to think about it. Let's see what happens," I said. I lifted the coffee pot and poured coffee into my cup and cut into my apple pie. I ended up applying for two jobs out of state, the one in Urbana and one in Cambridge. To my mother's pleasure, neither panned out.

My mother kept her job as a clerk in a doctor's office until she was seventy-five and she lived in my sister's building until the end of her life. She loved flowers and plants and would have been a gardener if she had had the chance. In Cabrini-Green she planted two rows of Rose of Sharon bushes along the perimeter

29

of our backyard. When we moved to Lake View the yard belonged to the landlord so she was limited to three indoor lily plants. Daisies were her favorite flower, whose simple white petals and cheerful yellow centers were a little bit like her: straightforward, uncomplicated, cheerful.

My mother also loved music. Her grandchildren played music— there was a clarinet-player (my sister's oldest son, Wesley), a flute-player (my daughter Lauren), and a trumpet player (my brother's oldest son, Mark)—at all of her birthday parties during the last twenty years of her life. They played her favorite song, In the Garden, a hymn we sang in church at Easter, three times, each kid playing it all the way through alone, standing in front of my mother, while my mother smiled and listened carefully, her eyes shining. My mother liked the popular music of her day too. I remember her listening to Johnny Mathis and Frank Sinatra on the radio in the kitchen in Cabrini-Green when I was a kid.

My mother never had a vacation my entire childhood and she never complained about that. When I was married and had my own kids we took her with us on two of our vacations, one of them to Cape Cod. We took a train to Boston and drove a rental car to our rented summer house in Sandwich on the Cape. We spent the week swimming in the ocean, sitting on the beach, having cookouts under the trees in the backyard, and going to the aquarium and the Union Oyster House, the oldest restaurant in continuous service in the U.S., in Boston. For a couple of hours during the twenty-three-hour train ride from Chicago to Boston, my daughters, Lauren and Kristen, who were eight and five at the time, stood in front of their seats and played house. They chattered back and forth, pretending that Lauren was the mother and Kristen was the baby. At one point my mother nudged me, pointed at the girls, and smiled broadly. Later she said watching them on the train was the most memorable part of the vacation for her. But she liked going to the New England Aquarium too.

My mother died on July 17, 2002, at the age of eighty. After all those years of working tirelessly her body finally gave out. First her heart and then the rest of her body started failing. She spent a couple of weeks in the hospital, then was taken to a nursing home. She died peacefully in her sleep in the early evening; my sister Ellyn was with her. Her funeral was held in the Devon Church of Jesus Christ, a non-denominational church in East Rogers Park, where we went when we were kids and where my mother went on Christmas and Easter till she was in her sixties. When people were filing in before the service, my sisters played a CD of some of my mother's favorite songs including Bridge Over Troubled Water by Simon and Garfunkel and You Can Close Your Eyes by James Taylor. First the minister spoke, then, one by one, three of my sisters, both of my brothers, and I got up and talked about my mother. I started out talking about the music my sisters chose to play at the beginning of the service. I told the story of how my mother's grandkids played the same song at her birthday parties for many years and how mother finally said, "I like In the Garden but it's not the only song I like."

I remember standing behind the podium, looking out at the people sitting in the half-filled church. I felt comfortable and comforted in this church: It was a church I had gone to for most of my life; I had been a Sunday school teacher here, a basketball coach on weekday nights and a counselor and director of their summer camp. I had even occasionally given sermons at this very podium when it was my turn to be the stand-in when the minister was on vacation.

I thought about my mother. I wanted to say something that would truly capture her spirit for these people sitting in this church. I had known many of them for many years, but most of them didn't know my mother, and I wanted to tell them something that would help them know her. And then it came to me what to say: My mother had a hard life, I said, but nothing ever kept her down. And that was what I learned from her. I learned many other things too: the value of hard work, what it means to make a family, how important it is to love your kids and show it. But probably the biggest lesson I learned from her is this:

Life will knock you down—it's not a matter of if but when. And when it does, what are you going to do? My mother taught me this: When life knocks you down, you get up.

Chapter 5

Poverty

My parents were married for over fifty years and had ten children. My mother did all the work of raising and taking care of the family because my father's alcoholism and arthritis cancelled out any ability he might have had to contribute. My mother was the hardest working person I've ever known. She cooked and cleaned for us all and worked every day from nine to five cleaning houses. She did all this while also putting up with my father. I'm still amazed that anyone could do all the things she did and never complain.

At least once a week my father took a bus to the tavern at six and came home at midnight in a cab. "Lucille, there's a cab down here," he yelled up the stairs when he came home drunk at night. My mother went out and paid the fare and then had to deal with a drunken husband. My older sisters told me that sometimes he hit her when he was drunk although I never witnessed that.

My father walked with a cane because he had arthritis. In college he'd been the captain of his football team, a member of Sigma Chi, a popular fraternity, a big man on campus at Illinois Wesleyan University. He graduated in 1929, during the Depression era when jobs were very hard to come by. He joined the Navy and served during World War II. After the Navy, he met my mother at the Edgewater Beach Hotel where they both worked, her as a maid and him as a waiter. If it hadn't been for his alcoholism, he might have been capable of holding a job despite his arthritis, but I don't remember him ever having a job.

Life in Cabrini would have been different if my father hadn't been an alcoholic. I would have gone to baseball games with him instead of to the tavern on Chicago Avenue, where I drank pop, ate candy, and played a video arcade game while he sat at the bar and drank beer, getting drunker and drunker. If he hadn't been an alcoholic, I thought, he would have had a job and we would have had a car. There would have been less tension in the family and we would have had better meals instead of the fried eggs and potatoes for dinner. We would have gone on family vacations and might not have lived in Cabrini at all.

My father always had his own room because nobody wanted to share one with him. In Cabrini, he had the bedroom at the end of the hallway while the rest of us slept three or four to a room in the other three bedrooms. After we moved to Lake View his room was an enclosed porch behind the bedroom I shared with my two brothers. It was at the far end of the apartment, separate from the other rooms. As soon as he saw it my father said, "This is perfect for me. It's going to be my cage." His years of getting drunk and abusive at least twice a month and not being able to hold down a job had created a divide between him and us, and he knew it. He spent his days lying on his cot and reading newspapers or watching television. His favorite was Gunsmoke and Festus, the stubble-faced deputy, and he sang along with Lawrence Welk. He liked tinkering with broken TVs and smoking Pall Mall cigarettes or White Owl cigars, in the cage. I told my friends he did this as a job because living on welfare never set right with me. He spent a lot of time on his typewriter corresponding with old friends from his alma mater, Illinois Wesleyan University, and his hometown, Virden, Illinois. They were his only friends.

Once when it was time to take the garbage out I found two trash bags sitting by the trash can in the kitchen instead of the usual one. As it turned out, one bag held garbage but the second bag didn't; it contained some of the television tubes my father used when he repaired TVs, which he did as a hobby, sitting in his room tinkering with the neighbors' broken TV sets. It was a Saturday morning when I took out the two bags of garbage and when my father woke up after drinking all night and discovered that I had thrown his television tubes away, he got mad as hell. He picked me up, an eight-year-old boy, and held me in the air and shook me.

"What the hell's wrong with you? Why you'd throw that bag away?" he yelled at me.

My second oldest sister, Ellyn, was in the living room. She heard him, ran into the kitchen, and screamed, "Put him down! Roger's job is to throw the garbage away and where were the television tubes? They were in a bag next to the garbage."

My father put me down and I was afraid of him ever since.

"Go outside and play," Ellyn said. I ran outside still crying, desperate to get away from my father. I could hear him yelling, "Who do you think you are?" at my sister before the screen door banged shut behind me. After that I avoided him even more than I had before.

We lived in Cabrini-Green because we were on welfare. My mother made fifteen dollars a day working five days a week as a maid even though it was against welfare regulations, and that helped put food on the table. My mother refused to accept the idea that we were poor and wouldn't apply for foodstamps. She always said we were comfortable not poor. But I think now that she was just proud and possibly in denial. My father didn't seem to mind living on welfare.

Being poor was embarrassing to me. I wore hand-me-downs, my brothers' old jeans and shirts, which were ragged and didn't fit that well. There were no organized activities like baseball or football in Cabrini-Green, but if there had been I wouldn't have been able to participate without a scholarship because we couldn't afford uniforms or registration fees. The only place I usually went outside our neighborhood was church. The times I did go somewhere that cost money, someone else had to pay for it. When I went to camp in the summer the church paid for it out of their scholarship fund, and when the Shriner circus came to town once a year Mr. Guibor, my mother's best friend's husband, bought the tickets for me and my sisters. The elephants and lions were my favorite acts. Someone else always having to pay for me made me feel shameful.

We had to take a bus or be picked up and driven whenever we went anywhere. A deacon usually picked me and my brothers and sisters up and drove us back and forth to church. My parents didn't go, except on Christmas when my mother came with us. At one point the deacon "got tired" of taking us to church and we stopped going until our pastor, Reverend Oyama, noticed we weren't there and asked someone why not, and then he started picking us up. The third time he drove us to church, the front passenger door flew open and I was thrown out of the car. I landed in the street, got up and brushed myself off and got back in—Reverend Oyama stopped as soon as I fell out, of course. He asked me if I was okay, I said I was, and we headed off again for church.

One day something happened that made me more aware than usual of how poor we were. Leo Edwards, one of the leaders of our church, picked me up for Awana in the church's blue station wagon. Awana was a global nonprofit Christian organization for youth. Our church had an Awana club that met once a week on Friday night at seven; my brothers had belonged to it too when they were younger and I went every week. When I answered the door that night Mr. Edwards said we would be going swimming at the Lawson YMCA instead of meeting at the church and it would cost 25 cents to use the pool. As usual, I didn't have any money, so I went to the kitchen and asked my mom for a quarter. She looked in her purse and didn't have one. I waited in the kitchen with Mr. Edwards while my mom went upstairs and asked two of my older sisters, Ellyn and Phyllis, who were studying in their bedroom, whether they had any money. Neither of them had 25 cents either. My mother came back downstairs and apologized dejectedly to Mr. Edwards. I was embarrassed, but not as embarrassed as my mom was. Mr. Edwards smiled and said he would pay for me tonight but I would have to pay him back. I nodded happily and ran upstairs to get my swim trunks.

She thanked Mr. Edwards and reminded me to behave. I glanced back at her as Mr. Edwards and I left the kitchen. I saw a look of humiliation in her eyes that I never forgot.

My oldest sister Aiko took me to a play downtown and dinner at the Pallidum Restaurant on Dearborn Street for my tenth birthday. That was the first time I went to a restaurant. A year later I would start eating out with the foreman at the polo ranch where I started working, but I never went to a restaurant with anybody in Cabrini either before or after that dinner with my sister.

There were four of us at the Pallidum: my sister Aiko, her good friend Sets, Sets' younger brother Bob, and me. When I walked into the restaurant I was impressed and a little intimidated by the white table cloths and red chairs. I followed my sister who followed the hostess to a table for four. When we sat down I copied everyone else and put my napkin on my lap. As I looked over the menu, my sister asked me what I wanted. She waited a minute or two and then suggested a steak and fries, which I ordered along with a Coke. When the food came I used my fork and knife at the same time to cut the steak—I knew how to do that because that's how we ate at home. Years later, when I was a teacher in the inner city of Chicago, I took a poor student to a restaurant for a meal and the knife and fork were like foreign objects to him, and I thought of that moment in Pallidum Restaurant, when I ate out for the first time on my tenth birthday.

My sister, Sets, and Bob talked about the play we'd just been to, Pinocchio. I listened, but mostly I looked around at all the white people sitting at tables eating and talking. I was around black people all the time and it was interesting to see so many white people in one place. At the end of dinner, my sister put a quarter next to my plate. When I stood up to leave I quietly put the quarter in my pocket. Sets saw me and told me to put it back on the table, explaining that it was a tip for the waitress. I reluctantly put the quarter back under the edge of my plate.

I blamed my father for our poverty and for most of our other problems. That was easy to do; when he drank he was mean and could sometimes be abusive. But there were times when my father was a nice man. He came out of his room on Thanksgiving and Christmas and cooked a turkey dinner. He was usually in a good mood then; at least he didn't yell at us, which was a relief. But I still steered clear of him. He rarely had a good thing to say to anybody.

On Christmas Day, at about eleven in the morning, he came out of his room, tied my mother's apron around his waist, and began cooking. He made turkey with stuffing, corn, mashed potatoes with gravy, and cranberry sauce. He'd learned how to cook during World War II, when he was a cook in the Navy. My older brothers pushed together the kitchen table and a long table somebody had given us—our father always called it the library table. My brothers set up our ping pong table—this was made of two sheets of plywood my father had clamped together—on top of the two tables so the surface would be large enough for all of us to eat around. My older sisters spread a white tablecloth over it and then set out plates, silverware and napkins. All ten kids, my parents, and sometimes a guest or two, such as my mother's best friend, Helen, or somebody from church who had nowhere else to go, sat around the table. My father said grace and then carved the turkey. We passed our plates to him and he dished some out onto each one and we passed around the rest of the food. We were all usually in a good mood and looking forward to opening presents. After dinner the table was cleared and we opened our presents and then played ping pong. I liked ping pong and got pretty good at it, but my older brothers and sisters usually won. My father didn't go to his bedroom right after dinner. He sat in the living room with his cane at his side and ate a piece of pie and watched us open our presents. My oldest sister Aiko had a job and her own apartment and she gave all of us kids new clothes wrapped with fancy Christmas wrapping paper. Her presents always looked expensive and they were. My mom started washing the dishes with my older sisters Phyllis and Donna's help.

Once, on the day after Christmas, my father told me and my younger sister Pat to go outside and look for a discarded Christmas tree still in good shape and take it to Mely and Molly's house. Mely and Molly were little girls, six and seven years old, who lived with their parents and their two-year-old brother Miguel in a row-house across the street from us. We didn't know them—we had seen Mely and Molly playing outside and heard other kids calling their names—but we had no more than a passing acquaintance with them at best, and I felt strange looking for a Christmas tree to bring them the day after Christmas. As far as I know my father didn't know them either and I still don't understand why he told us to do that. Maybe he knew they had nothing and he thought a Christmas tree was something.

Pat and I found a tree with a little tinsel hanging off the branches, sitting on the side of the street two rowhouses over. We dragged it along the street to Molly and Mely's house and knocked on their door. Mely answered wearing a plaid dress and with her hair up in a pony tail. Standing in the little foyer, I could see her mother and Molly and Miguel looking startled in the living room, as if they couldn't imagine who would be at their door. I asked Mely if she wanted the Christmas tree. She looked at her mom and her mom nodded and we carried the tree into the house and left it on the living room floor. The house was cold and there wasn't even a chair to sit down on. My sister and I didn't say anything as we walked back home, but I thought about that empty house and the poverty that was palpable in it. I didn't feel poor any more.

Chapter 6
Outside the Projects

When I was in third grade my mom's best friend, Helen, who lived in a rowhouse two blocks away from us, got married to Mr. Guibor. Mr. Guibor was an old man with gray hair who always wore a suit and tie and was an executive at Holoway, the candy factory that made Milk Duds. Helen was his secretary and he fell in love with her. They got married and Helen was able to move out of Cabrini. After Helen married Mr. Guibor she hired my mom to clean her house every week, and one Saturday when I was in fifth grade my mom asked me if I wanted to go with her. She cleaned a different house every day, and she would never have invited me along to anywhere else, but she knew Helen wouldn't mind. I think my mom wanted to spend time with me and show me the world outside of Cabrini.

Helen and Mr. Guibor lived in a brown brick bungalow in a quiet neighborhood on Wilson, a tree - lined street that crossed the Chicago River five miles north of Cabrini-Green. To get there my mom and I took the Chicago Avenue bus to the train station and then took the Ravenswood train and got off at the Wilson stop. From there we walked three blocks to Helen's house, crossing a bridge over the Chicago River. Even though it was the same river as the one that flowed through Cabrini, it looked and felt completely different here. The air smelled fresher and the sound of birds filled the air. This river was lined with trees and had small speedboats docked at a long pier jutting out from the shore. The river in Cabrini had train tracks running along beside it and four huge pale blue-salt mountains beside the tracks. Once my brothers Robert and Billy and my friend Milton and I walked across the bridge to the salt mountains and ran up and down them; then we saw a security guard approaching, driving along the railroad tracks toward us, and we ran away.

Helen's house was one block from the river. My mother rang the bell and Helen opened the door and hugged my mom and then me and we all went into the kitchen and sat at the table. I had a glass of orange juice and my mom and Helen drank coffee. They talked and talked and I got bored. I knew I was there to help clean but since they were just talking I asked my mom if I could go outside. She said I could for a little while, but to come back in half an hour because that's when she would start working.

I walked up and down the block, past brick ranches, bunga-lows, and green lawns. Parked cars lined both sides of the street. I was thrilled to be walking around, exploring the neighborhood. This was one of the first times I'd been outside of Cabrini, other than church. I walked to the river and saw a man and woman preparing to take a speedboat out on the water. I stood and watched the man untie the rope and then start the engine while the woman wearing a red visor sat on the seat in the back and looked at the sailboat gliding past. The man steered the boat down the river at a slow pace. Then I walked back to Helen's house.

I rang the bell and my mom opened the door. "It's time for work," she said. She had a navy-blue-and-white plaid apron tied around her waist and there were beads of sweat on her forehead. Her wavy black hair was pushed back away from her forehead with a red bandana. She curled her hair every Saturday night, wrapping the strands around pink plastic rollers and watching TV with her feet up on a brown naugahyde ottoman. Standing in Helen's doorway waiting for me to come in and help her clean, she seemed content, maybe even happy, not tired or hurried. "How was your walk? Helen went shopping and might not be back before we leave."

"It's nice out here. I saw a man take off on his speedboat. That was cool. The Chicago River looks different here. What do you want me to do?"

"It's different from Cabrini. You can go back outside when you're finished but now go in the kitchen and sweep the floor. Do a good job now. When you're done with sweeping I'll show you where the garbage goes and you can take it out." After telling me what to do she went back to vacuuming the living room. I was happy to sweep the kitchen floor and take the garbage out. My mom vacuumed and cleaned the two bedrooms and bathrooms. After taking out the garbage I offered to help clean a bathroom but my mom told me I could go outside and so I did. As it turned out I spent more time exploring this new Chicago river and Helen's neighborhood than I did working.

We finished cleaning the house before Helen got home. On the walk to the train we stopped at a small grocery store and my mom bought us both a bottle of pop and an ice cream cone. As we sat on the train eating our ice cream I remember her saying she hoped we didn't see anyone we knew because she said she felt like a kid eating ice cream and drinking a pop. Sitting on the train next to my mom with an ice cream cone and a bottle of orange crush I was as happy as I could be.

Chapter 7

Summer Camp

I ran into the water from the sandy shore. The boys who could swim raced to the pier and dove into the water. The sun was shining but the water was cold for an August day. At lunch, our counselor William Hong, said,

"I can take all you guys on. You won't get me under."

All seven of us boys made a bond with each other as we looked across the table at each other.

"You're going down," we chanted.

William was in his early twenties, six feet tall, and wore glasses. He slept in my cabin with me and six other boys. The campground was on the shores of Lake Geneva in southern Wisconsin, right over the Illinois border. It was a Christian camp on 21 acres of rolling hills and trees. There were eleven green wooden cabins at the camp in all. The cabins rested at the bottom of a hill that we climbed three times a day to get to the Mess Hall for our meals. We went to the soda fountain in the basement of the administration building at night for ice cream and candy, we called it the canteen. We went fishing in the morning and swimming in the lake in the afternoon.

We walked down the hill back to our cabin. Before swimming we had arts and crafts. I was making a dark brown leather keychain and hoped to have it done by Saturday. I couldn't wait to dunk our counselor. When arts and crafts ended I ran to my cabin and changed into my swim trunks. The other guys were right beside me.

I left my towel in the cabin and ran out to the lake. When I got waist high in the cold water I dove in. The guys who could swim jumped in off the pier. Our counselor took his time walking to the lake and slowly waded in. He knew what was coming. I jumped on his back, put my arms around his neck and pulled with all my might trying to get him down under water. He reached his arm behind him, grabbed me and threw me three feet in the air and I splashed into the cold water. William threw two other boys into the water but we kept coming back for more. I looked across the lake and saw four older boys in canoes beyond the pier. One of them, Chester, stood up in the canoe, took off his t-shirt and dove in. Some girls in red and yellow kayaks laughed and then one girl jumped in and joined Chester.

I was determined to dunk William. I jumped on his back again and pulled with all my might. This time Jeffrey, my cabin mate, was also on William's back pulling and pulling and we finally got him down into the water. When he went under we all cheered. In three seconds he was on his feet looking for more action. He wiped his hands across his face and the top of his head. I tried getting away but I couldn't. He grabbed me and threw me. I flew through the air and landed with a splash five feet away from him and water went up my nose. Forty minutes later we were all tired after wrestling with William and ready to quit. We walked out of the water and headed back to the cabin to dry off and change clothes. We dried off and put our shorts and t shirts back on. We hung around the cabin and talked until it was time to march out to the field for revelry before marching up the hill for chow.

We started the morning by making our beds, sweeping the floor of the cabin, and checking the corners for cobwebs. We did this every day. The camp director inspected the cabins every day while we were eating breakfast. The cleanest cabin got points. There were points for Bible memorization and winning at kickball and softball too, and the cabin with the most points total won a trophy at the end of the week.

After cleaning our cabin we marched out to the end of the field for flag raising, the Pledge of Allegiance, and the camp director's prayer. One of the older campers played revelry; he played taps when it was time to turn the lights off at night.

After the morning flag raising we marched up the hill for breakfast, and after breakfast we had a Bible lesson. I liked the daily Bible lessons; they made me think about God and how happy I was to be here, surrounded by trees and near a lake. Before each lesson we sang spiritual songs like How Great Thou Art and also fun songs like Gunk Gunk went the Little Green Frog. In the afternoon we played kickball and soccer, made braided lanyards and painted water-color pictures of boats on the lake, and went swimming. Everyone was polite most of the time, and the counselors made sure no one was left out of any games and activities.

The week went quickly. On Wednesday night I bought a postcard in the lobby of the administration building and mailed it to my mom. Thursday night was performance night. Every cabin had to perform a cheer that they came up with and the winning cheer got points. My cabin made up a cheer that went, We went down to the river, yeah man and started to drown yeah man. But when I thought about those Braves, yeah man, I just couldn't go down. The cabins were named after baseball teams and we were the Braves. Our performance was a little lackluster—cheering wasn't really our cup of tea—and some of the other cabins yelled louder and showed more excitement than we did and got more points that night.

There was a ceremony on Friday night where the camp director, Mr. Craig, announced the winner of the trophy. The Dodgers, the cabin where the oldest boys lived, won the trophy. The winners yelled and jumped around and hugged each other. My friends and I smiled at each other and shrugged. We were a little disappointed but we hadn't expected to win.

I felt like crying on Saturday afternoon when it was time to leave. I remember sitting in the church van with tears in my eyes as people stood in the parking lot waving good-bye. When I got home, I played camp for a week. I pretended to be the song leader with pretend campers sitting on the living room floor in front of me. I became a Christian at this camp the summer after my senior year in high school.

Chapter 8

The Polo Ranch

Sometimes on Saturday afternoons I went grocery shopping with my mother, pulling the cart along the sidewalk on Larrabee Street to the A&P. I remember going with her once on a late-summer Saturday evening, when school had already started. Walking to the store took us out of the projects for an hour or two. My mom asked me about school and my friends. I told her my fifth grade teacher was stricter than my 4th grade teacher and gave us work more.

In the store I pushed the cart and my mom pulled out her list and pointed the cart in the direction of aisle 3. In aisle 3 she grabbed a box of Cheerios and a box of Frosted Flakes, my favorite, and put them in the cart. We wheeled the cart to the dairy section and picked up a gallon of milk and a quart of buttermilk for my father. My father was the only one who drank buttermilk—the rest of us couldn't stand it; it was thick and creamy and hard to swallow. Before long the cart was filled with grocery, including ten pounds of potatoes and two dozen eggs. My mother made fried eggs and potatoes at least twice a week, for dinner, not for breakfast. The last thing we did in the A&P was pick up five pounds of hamburger and two loaves of bread. My mom put a half gallon of chocolate ice cream in the cart without any pleading from me. She always tried to give us kids a little something special. An ice cream truck was sitting in the parking lot when we came out of the store and my mom gave me a dime and told me to buy myself something. I ordered a chocolate ice cream cone and handed the guy, who was wearing a white paper hat, my money, and my mom and I took turns pulling the shopping cart filled with bags of groceries so I could eat my ice cream cone before it melted.

The cool breeze felt good against my skin as I licked the ice cream that dripped down the sides of the cone. I decided to pick this time to ask my mother something I had been thinking about for a while.

"Do you think I could get a job at the polo ranch?" My two older brothers, Billy and Robert, had been working at the polo ranch during the summer and on the weekends for four and five years respectively. The ranch foreman picked them up on Monday evening and brought them home in time for dinner on the following Sunday, all summer long until school started in September. During the school year he picked them up on Friday and brought them back on Sunday. "What do they do there?" I asked my mother now.

She told me they cleaned horse stalls and saddles and bridles and made sure the horses were ready to ride during the polo games. The polo games were in Oakbrook and the ranch was in Hinsdale, two southern suburbs of Chicago. Billy and Robert slept in a cabin on the ranch and had their meals at nearby restaurants.

"I want to work there too and make some money," I said.

My mom looked at me, surprised. I was only ten, and my brothers hadn't started

working at the polo ranch until they were twelve. "There's no rush," my mom said, smiling.

I finished my ice cream cone and took over pulling the cart the rest of the way home. When we reached Hudson Street, two blocks from our house, we were back in the projects.

I started working on the polo ranch the following summer, just before seventh grade.

The alarm clock blared at 6 a.m. My older brother Billy shook me and told me we had to get up and feed the horses before breakfast. It was my first day of work at the polo ranch. Last night Herman, my new boss, picked up Billy and me and drove us to the ranch. I looked out the car window and grew excited about this new adventure, working on the polo ranch.

Billy took me to the white wood-framed cabin I'd be sharing with him. The cabin was small, with only room enough for two twin beds, one dresser, and a nightstand with a lamp and a clock radio on it. There was a little black and white TV on top of the dresser. Herman slept in the other cabin on the ranch. There were forty acres on the ranch. Along with the barns and the two workers' cabins there were corrals, a big field where the owner and his two sons practiced playing polo, and an apple orchard. The owner and his wife lived in the big white house we had passed when on the way in.

I got out of bed, threw on some jeans and a t-shirt, and went outside with Billy. He showed me how to feed and water the horses. Billy pulled a hose to one of the horse stalls and started filling the metal water bucket. He gave me the hose and told me to do the rest. After watering the horses, Billy and I pulled a wheelbarrow of oats to each stall and poured a can of oats into the food box while all the horses pawed the ground anxiously waiting to be fed. Billy told me I'd be feeding and watering the horses by myself from now on while he did other early-morning chores. I would come to enjoy feeding the horses. It made me feel like I was accomplishing something and I liked horses.

When the horses were fed and watered Billy and I piled into Herman's blue Chevy and drove four miles to the Fifth Wheel truck stop for breakfast. Semi-trucks and cars were parked in the lot outside the Fifth Wheel. Inside, the place smelled of cigarette smoke and was crowded with truck drivers and some locals. We followed Herman to one of the round tables in the middle of the room and the waitress smiled and brought Herman a cup of coffee as soon as we sat down. He smoked a cigarette and drank coffee while we looked at the menu. For the first time in my life I could have anything I wanted from the menu. I looked around the restaurant and saw old people hunched over their pancakes and talking with their mouths half full. The thought of getting anything I wanted didn't drive me to read the menu but instead brought on an urge for a chocolate donut. So when the waitress took our orders I ordered a chocolate donut and a glass of orange juice. Billy and Herman ordered bacon and eggs. Billy sopping up his egg yolks with toast and Herman drinking a second cup of coffee. "What do we have going today?" asked Billy.

"The usual." Herman said. "Cleaning stalls when we get back and then we'll see from there. The saddles have to be cleaned and I hope to get an order of wood shavings for the stalls this week." I would be starving at lunchtime after a morning of hard work cleaning stalls, and I realized then that a chocolate donut wasn't enough and from then on I ordered bacon and eggs, like Billy and Herman.

When we got back to the ranch we all cleaned stalls. The horses needed clean, dry wood shavings, which were good for their hooves. Herman drove the tractor and pulled the manure spreader from stall to stall and he also cleaned every third stall while Billy and I cleaned the others. We went from stall to stall and cleaned each one, using pitchforks to shovel dirty and wet wood shavings into the manure spreader while the horse stood to the side of the stall. I got use to the foul smell of manure but after the fifth stall I could hardly lift my arms and sweat dripped off my body. I worked at the ranch three summers in a row. It was hard work and low pay, but it got me out of the projects and I liked making money. Shoveling manure into the spreader never got easier.

We cleaned stalls for the first half of the morning and then took a twenty-minute break. I sat in a green metal chair outside the tack room and drank fruit punch from the Kraml Dairy—Mr. Kraml, who owned the polo ranch, also owned Kraml Dairy. Herman and Billy smoked a cigarette and had a can of Coke. Herman would spend the rest of the workday riding horses to give them exercise. I would clean saddles the rest of the day. Standing in the tack room sponging down the drity saddles, I watched him put on the saddles and bridles and ride the magnificent horses from the barns down to the field and gallop around the grass until the horse worked up a white sweat, getting in shape for the polo matches. I wanted to change places with Herman. Herman grumbled about riding horses most of the day. I was stuck cleaning tack (saddles and bridles) in the tack room. I washed every saddle and bridle in the tack room with saddle soap and water, sponging them down until they shone. It kept the leather clean and soft. I did this every day, all afternoon, while Billy replaced the dirty wood shavings we'd shoveled out of the stalls, with new clean shavings.

Some afternoons we went to polo matches in Oak Brook. I sat in the front seat with Herman while he drove the long horse-trailer to the polo fields. Herman led the horses to and from the matches and I sponged them down and then walked the hot sweaty horses as they cooled down after their periods. Polo game days were my favorites, though it would be a good month before I went to one of them. When I was at the polo games I looked around at the people sitting in lawn chairs next to their mercedes benz drinking beer or a glass of wine and applauding on the occasion of a score. This was how rich people lived I thought and I looked at them with envy wishing I had a Coke.

It was like my mother said, we would go to restaurants and fast food places for all of our meals. We always ate breakfast at the restaurant, had lunch in the car, and carry-out for dinner.

For lunch on my first day we went to Dog and Suds and Chicken Unlimited for dinner. Herman paid for all the meals and was reimbursed by Mr. Kraml. My pay was twenty dollars a week plus room and board. On my second Tuesday morning, when Herman handed me my first check, I looked at the number on the amount line and saw eighteen dollars and fifty cents. I asked Herman why I wasn't getting twenty dollars and he said Uncle Sam had to take his share. I laid the pitchfork against the stall wall and stared at my check with tears in my eyes. On the following Monday, my day off—Herman always picked me up on Monday night and dropped me off on Sunday at suppertime, sometimes he'd stay for Sunday dinner. The first Monday, me and my mom took a bus downtown to First Federal Savings and

Loan and opened an account with my first check. I wasn't saving for anything in particular. I opened the bank account because I thought I was expected to. Ten years later I used my savings, $2,000.00 to buy a new car, a green 1973 stick-shift Chevy Vega.

Billy only worked on the ranch for a few weeks, during my first summer there, and after that he went to summer school. After he left I was alone there with Herman. I stayed at the polo ranch for three years. For the first two years I took a week off in August to go to Camp Lake Chi Co. I quit my job at the polo ranch one year after we moved to Lake View and started working as a bagger at National, a grocery store a block from my new house. After I had been working on the ranch for two years, Mr. Kraml invited me to sleep in his house on the weekends during the school year. There was an empty bedroom because his two sons hadn't lived there for years and now had their own families. Mr. Kraml started talking about wanting to adopt me but I didn't pay much attention. Once he called my mother and told her he wanted to adopt me. My mother wasn't very happy about that idea, but she told me she'd leave it up to me. I told her I wasn't interested in being adopted by Mr. Kraml.

When I slept in the Kramls' house on weekends during the school year, Mrs. Kraml left out cold cereal and milk for my breakfast and made me bologna sandwiches for lunch. I don't think she particularly wanted to feed me and I missed going out to the restaurants with Herman.

Mr. Kraml invited me to have dinner with his family twice. The second time we went to the Country Kitchen, owned by Mr. Kraml's sister, and the first time we ate in Mr. Kraml's screened-in porch at a big glass table that seated ten. Mr. Kraml's son Ken cooked steaks and chicken on the grill outside. When we sat down to eat, Mr. Kraml said, "Welcome to our table, Roger. It's good to have you joining us." He picked up his fork, looked down the table at me, and reminded me to put my napkin on my lap. I felt my face get red. I knew proper etiquette and I knew that you should keep your napkin on your lap when you ate. When Mr. Kraml told me to do that I felt like even more of an outsider at that big glass table, even more like I didn't belong there, and I started crying and I couldn't stop. Mr. Kraml tried to explain that he hadn't meant to embarrass me but it didn't help. I finally stopped crying and ate my dinner. I couldn't turn down a bowl of ice cream and when I finished dessert Mr. Kraml told me I could leave. I walked around the ranch, to the barns and over to the apple orchard, thinking about the disaster I'd created at dinner and how I didn't fit in. I felt embarrassed and ashamed and homesick. Mr. Kraml never invited me to eat dinner at his house again.

Even though I was glad I didn't have to eat dinner with the Kraml's, eating by myself was the worst thing about the job. Herman usually drove into the city to see his girlfriend—he liked fat women and his girlfriend must've weighed 250 pounds—in the evening, and sometimes he didn't come back until morning. I sat in my cabin and ate chicken or an Italian beef sandwich and watched television. Friday Night at the Movies was my favorite TV show. I leaned back against a pillow resting on the headboard of my single bed and watched Spartacus or The Magnificent Seven or Elmer Gantry. To break things up I went outside and walked around the ranch, tossing apples I found on the ground in the orchard, seeing if I could hit a tree from twenty yards away.

During my last summer working on the ranch, I took a horse out once a week for an evening ride. I never asked anyone if I could do it and nobody knew I was doing it, except once, when Mr. Kraml saw me riding a horse around the corral. One night I put a saddle and bridle on Hickory, a horse with a calm disposition, thinking we would walk down to the field and canter a bit. I jumped in the saddle and Hickory walked placidly down the hill, but when he saw the open field he took off at a gallop. I leaned forward and clung to his neck, terrified and hanging on for dear life. Then all of a sudden he stopped galloping. We turned around and I jumped down, took the reins, and walked him back to the stable. In the stable I took off his tack and put him back in his stall. I was ready for television.

At the beginning of that summer my friend Sam from school came out for a week to work at the ranch. It was the summer after my freshman year in high school, when I had been living in Lake View for two years. One day in woodshop I told Sam about working at the ranch. He said it sounded like fun and then said, "Can I go?" I checked with Herman and he said it was fine if Sam came and worked on the ranch. Having him there made the week go by fast. He helped me water the horses and clean the stalls, and in the evening we walked the ranch and had contests to see who could hit the most trees with apples. On Sunday night, when we were waiting for Herman to drive us home, Sam said the work was too hard and he didn't want to come back. I quit the job two weeks later. I wanted to stay in the city with my friends, and I was tired of being by myself so much. My mother called Mr. Kraml to tell him I didn't want to work at the ranch any more, and he told her he was very disappointed and asked to speak with me on the phone. I was standing next to my mother in the dining room and she held the phone away and told me Mr. Kraml wanted to talk to me. But I didn't want to talk to him—I felt guilty about quitting and disappointing this man who had wanted to adopt me and take me to Florida when the Kramls played polo there in the winter, and I didn't want to deal with his hurt feelings or listen to him to try to talk me out of my decision—so I shook my head and my mother told him I wouldn't come to the phone.

Chapter 9

Last Hot Dog at Sammy's

My friend Lorenzo and I walked to Sammy's for lunch. It was my last day at Cooley Junior High, and I had mixed feelings about leaving. I was excited about moving but also kind of sad. I'd known some of the kids in my class since first grade. Cabrini was the only home I'd ever known, and I'd always thought I'd be living here until I turned eighteen and moved out on my own like my oldest sister. Now I realized there was a good chance I'd never see Lorenzo or my other friends in Cabrini again. As it turned out, I was right. I've missed Lorenzo over the years and have often wondered what happened to him.

There was a short line at Sammy's and the smell of burgers and fries made me hungry. I ordered my usual, a hot dog with mustard and relish, fries, and a coke.

"You're going to miss Sammy's, aren't you, Rog," Lorenzo said, sipping his drink. "What's your new neighborhood like? Bet it doesn't have as many black people."

"I'll miss Sammy's for sure and you maybe. I don't know much about my new neighborhood.—I haven't been there yet. Finish your burger. I don't want to be late on my last day." I sat on a stool and looked at cars drive pass on Division Street. I won't be doing this ever again I thought with a hint of regret.

"It's your last day so what if you're late."

"I know, but let's head back anyway."

Lorenzo finished his burger. We tossed our garbage and headed back to school. A block away from the school we ran into a group of high school boys who were standing along the sidewalk. One of them stepped right in front of me and I stopped. "What are you doing here, white boy?" he said looking straight at me.

"What do you think he's doing here? He's here just like you and me," Lorenzo said, stepping up next to me. "You think he'd be here if he didn't have to be?"

"You Frankie's little brother?" one of the other bullies said to Lorenzo.

"Yeah. Frankie's my brother," said Lorenzo.

"All right."

The boy standing in front of me got out of my way. "I better not see you around here again," he said.

You won't, I thought but didn't say. I started walking away and Lorenzo followed me. "Thanks, man," I said to Lorenzo when we were out of earshot of the bullies. "I can't believe this happened on my last day."

"Don't pay any attention to them," said Lorenzo.

Easy for him to say, I thought. I thought of how I had seen a tall Hispanic high school boy with long wavy black hair getting hit in the face over and over again by a group of black high school boys in the front of the school during the first week. I didn't know him but I felt sorry for him and I felt doubly glad I had a friend like Lorenzo. I didn't see the Hispanic kid around after the first week of school.

I felt relieved but still nervous all the way back to school. We made it there in time for afternoon classes.

I went up to Mr. Wilson at the end of math class and gave him my book. Mr. Wilson had had my older brother Robert as well as me as his students and he told me he wished us both well. When I heard that I was jolted once again by the reality that we were moving.

In homeroom at the end of the day, when we were lined up along the wall waiting for the bell to ring, Mr. Grant, my homeroom teacher, announced in a loud voice, "You know today is Mr. Prosise's last day with us. He'll be starting at a new school on Monday. We'll certainly miss Roger and we wish him the best."

I looked down at the floor, embarrassed by the attention. There were a few moments of silence and then someone started clapping and the rest of the class joined in. I looked around the room at the kids I'd known for so many years—some good friends of mine, some just kids I'd gone to school with day after day, year after year—all of them clapping, smiling at me, and I thought of how much I would miss them.

When the bell rang we shuffled out of the room, walked down the hall, and exited through the side door onto Division Street. The sky was blue and the afternoon air was cool though still a bit warm for an autumn day. Lorenzo and I stood on the sidewalk looking at each other, not knowing what to say.

"I'll miss you, good luck," said Lorenzo with a half smile. He turned and headed toward home.

"Same here, man. See you," I called after him, and then I crossed Division Street and walked home from Cooley for the last time. As I passed by the red-brick high rises I wondered what my new neighborhood would look like. What will it be like living around so many white people, I wondered. After the high rises I came to the rowhouses where I had lived my whole life. These rowhouses would soon be a part of my past.

When I got home I watched Leave it to Beaver on television and then went outside. There were five of us boys, enough for a game of touch football. My friend Milton could throw the ball the farthest so he was the designated quarterback for both teams. Karl and I played against Glen and Lamont. Lamont was the fastest boy and he caught a lot of passes. Karl tried guarding him first and then me. He was too fast for both of us. Glen and Lamont won the game but it was still fun. We played until it started to get dark and then everyone went home. My friends didn't know I was moving until the truck arrived the next morning. I never said anything to my friends because I wasn't one hundred percent sure it would happen.

At home I went to my room and packed my clothes in a duffle bag left over from my father's time in the Navy. We had chicken pot pies for dinner and then watched The Days of Wine and Roses on Friday Night at the Movies. Most of the work of moving would come the next day, Saturday. My brothers and sisters and I would load the truck with all of our stuff.

Part II
Lake View

Chapter 10

Have a Seat Next to Harold

"Have a seat right there in the front next to Harold," my new homeroom teacher, Mr. Jones, told me in a loud voice, pointing to an empty stool at the front table in the first row.

I looked around the room. The periodic table was stapled to a bulletin board in the back. A kid in the last row glanced at me as he walked to the pencil sharpener near the window. There were three rows of tables with black marble tops, a stool on either side of the table, and a sink in the middle of it. The room was similar to my science room in seventh grade at Cooley, except that back then when I looked around the room I saw all black faces. Now when I looked around the room I saw almost all white faces.

I sat in the first row at the first table next to a boy whose name, I would soon find out, was Harold Doyle. He would be the second Harold I'd met in this new neighborhood; the other Harold, the one I hit the night before last when he pushed John in front of our apartment, was a year younger than this Harold. This Harold smiled and said hi. He had black hair combed straight back away from his forehead and wore a black plaid long-sleeve shirt. To my surprise he stuck his hand out and shook mine; eighth grade kids didn't usually shake hands, and I thought Harold must be a good guy. Later I learned that he was in the local gang, the MGs—the name arose from the fact that most of the members lived near Magnolia and Grace streets. I also learned that the MG members drank and started fights in the schoolyard at night. But Harold was always friendly and polite to me.

I glanced out the window. The room was on the third floor. When I sharpened my pencil near the windows a few minutes later I saw cars on the street and people on the sidewalk below.

"Roger Prosise, am I pronouncing that right?" asked Mr. Jones. I learned later that Mr. Jones was in charge of Friday Night Social Center and the spring softball tournament.

"Prosise," I replied, emphasizing the long i as in the word 'ice.'

"We have a test today," Mr. Jones said, walking behind the teacher's table in the front of the room. "I hope you knuckleheads studied," he said, addressing the class. He was bald except for a line of salt-and-pepper hair on the sides of his head and he was wearing a white shirt and red tie. "I know it's your first day but take the test anyway, Prosise. It won't count toward your grade."

Mr. Jones passed out the test and reviewed the instructions, noting that some questions were worth more points than others. The test was three pages and had twenty-five questions worth a total of 100 points. I looked over the test and noticed that the answers to a lot of the questions had been covered in the notes Mike gave me on Saturday night, and that three of the questions were about the scientific method. I had memorized the steps of the scientific method when I was studying Mike's notes in our living room on Sunday afternoon.

The room was quiet. Mr. Jones remained behind his table. I read through the test again before beginning. Then I answered most of the questions, leaving a few I didn't know the answers to blank. I finished the test with five minutes left in the forty-minute period. I felt good about how I had done, especially since it was my first day and the test wouldn't count. I would have bombed if I hadn't studied Mike's notes on the weekend.

When the period was over I followed the class to social studies with Mrs. Cohen. In that room the desks were arranged in groups of four. Mrs. Cohen lectured for ten minutes and then we worked on an assignment, answering questions about the

American Revolution in the book. This turned out to be how the class went pretty much every day; social studies was a lot like English.

After class I saw Mike, Eddie, and Johnny in the hall and said hi to them. They were in different homerooms than I was. There were four eighth grade homerooms at Blaine. Mrs. Hoffman's homeroom, as I would later learn, was for the smartest kids. Mrs. Lee's room was for the next to the smartest kids. Mike was in Mrs. Hoffman's room. Johnny and Eddie were in Mrs. Cohen's room at the lowest end of the spectrum. Mr. Jones's homeroom was for the kids considered second from the bottom. I was in Mr. Jones's room. Years later, when I was an adult and a school superintendent, it came to me that I had probably been put in Mr. Jones's homeroom because I was transferring from Cabrini-Green -- that the principal or whoever made that decision at Blaine didn't expect me to be very bright or well prepared. What happened to high expectations?

In math with Mrs. Hoffman we took turns solving long-division problems at the board. I solved my problem in less than a minute and sat at my desk and watched in surprise as four of the other students struggled.

After math we had lunch. I walked across the street and ate lunch at home. My father made bologna sandwiches for me and my three younger sisters, Pat, Annette, and Linda. Just a week ago, lunch at school meant a walk to a hot dog stand and taking the chance of getting beat up. My sisters and I didn't talk much as we ate. We all wanted to go back to school and play with our new friends. When the bell rang in the schoolyard I got in line but I didn't run to get there like the younger kids did.

For the rest of that first day, I followed the class from room to room and teacher to teacher. I checked out the girls and noticed some cute ones. After school I changed into a t-shirt and gym shoes, then did my homework at the library table in the living room. My father came out of his room and tried to start a conversation.

"How do you like your new school? What are you working on?"

I had no interest in making small talk with him. This was the man who had beaten me and my siblings when he was drunk. He would never drink alcohol again—he stopped cold turkey when we moved to Lake View—but I didn't know that that would happen yet and even if I had known it wouldn't have erased the past. "It's okay," I said turning my head toward him. "Social studies. I have to answer five questions."

" I liked social studies when I was a kid. What kind of questions? Do you like social studies?"

"I don't know."

"What do you mean you don't know?" I turned around in my chair and saw my father standing in the kitchen hallway with his cane, looking across the dining room at me with a half smile and a hopeful look in his eyes. When I look back on this moment now I realize that he was reaching out to me, but I was stubborn and unforgiving. That wasn't the only time he reached out and I pushed him away. In high school when I was on the football team, he came to two of my games and I didn't run over to the stands and say hi to him even after my friend Rich told me to. Even though I shunned him, he still made arrangements for me to get a scholarship to his alma mater, Illinois Wesleyan University in Bloomington, Illinois. I didn't accept the scholarship because I wanted to go to another school, but I felt proud of the fact that other kids and my coaches knew that Illinois Wesleyan was interested in me.

"Alright. I give up," he said. "I tried." He turned and walked back to the kitchen and got a glass of water from the sink.

I finished my homework and went to my bedroom. I knew my father was back in his room, the room he called his cage. I pictured him there lying on the cot reading the newspaper. He stayed in his room most of the time. I put my book and papers on the desk in my room and turned around and left the apartment.

I ran down the stairs hoping to find Mike and go over to the schoolyard. I was getting used to having a schoolyard right across the street. Mike wasn't out in front of our building so I ran over to the schoolyard alone where some kids were playing basketball and football. Mike was playing football so I joined that group. We made two teams and played touch. Two high school kids were there and they played quarterback. I was a receiver and caught two touchdown passes. I ran faster than most of the guys. In Cabrini I was good at sports but in Lake View I was even better.

Afterwards Mike and I and some of the other guys sat on the porch of our apartment building. My new friends told me about the social center again and asked me if I wanted to go this Friday evening. There would be ping-pong and bumper pool and dancing in the gym. I'd played ping-pong and bumper pool at the afternoon social center at Jenner School, but I had never been to a dance, which was the part that intrigued me the most.

I went upstairs for dinner at around six. Five people could sit at our kitchen table and there were seven kids living at home so we had to eat in shifts, but it worked out because we all had different schedules. My older sisters and brothers were in high school and college and had part-time jobs so they ate at different times almost every night, depending on their schedule.

Tonight my mom ate standing at the counter, and I sat at the kitchen table with my sisters Donna, Pat, Annette and Linda. We all listened to my younger sister Annette tell my mom that kids in her class threw paper airplanes around the room and the class assignments were easy. I told my mom my day went fine and I was making friends. We had meatloaf and mashed potatoes. I poured a small puddle of ketchup on my meatloaf; I loved ketchup on meatloaf.

"Did you have the science test?" asked Mom.

"Yeah. The teacher said it wouldn't count but I'm still glad I studied Mike's notes. I think I did okay."

I finished eating and then did my chores. Just like in Cabrini I had to sweep the kitchen floor and take out the garbage, only now the garbage went in a fifty-gallon steel drum twenty yards behind our new apartment. My sisters were sitting on the sofa watching Laugh-In. Lily Tomlin was on as Ernestine the tele-phone operator and my sisters laughed hard at everything she said.

I took the garbage out the back door then ran out front look-ing for Mike. I caught up with him on the corner and we ran to the schoolyard and shot baskets with a few other kids for about an hour. Then we went back home and shot the breeze on the porch for a bit. He told me his birthday was next weekend and his mom had said he could have a sleepover and I was invited. His parents hardly ever let him have sleepovers but he told his mom that it would be a good way for me to make more friends so she let him. Mike wanted to hear more about Cabrini-Green. We sat on the steps and one of the things I told him was that I had never stayed over at anyone's house in Cabrini.

I went upstairs at around nine-thirty, joined my sisters on the couch, and watched the end of The Big Valley. When the news came on at ten I took a shower, brushed my teeth, and put on my pajamas. Then I went back out to the living room and watched Johnny Carson with my older sisters and brothers. They thought Johnny Carson was the funniest man alive. I didn't think he was very funny and after the third time of saying so my brother told me to go to bed.

Chapter 11

The Science Test

"I have your test results to hand back this morning. There was only one surprise: The student who started yesterday got the highest score in the class. Roger Prosise got a score of 85. Can someone tell me how a boy who wasn't even in class got a higher score than you knuckleheads who've been sitting in front of me all year? Even more, what does that say about my teaching?"

I was shocked and elated to hear that I'd gotten the highest score in the class.

Harold stared at me and said, "You must be a smart son of a bitch."

I looked back at him, smiled, and said, "Thanks."

The class was silent and in a state of disbelief like me. Mr. Jones passed back the tests.

"You don't belong in this class, Roger," he announced when he was finished reviewing the answers to each question with the class. "Harold, walk Roger down to Mrs. Hoffman's classroom."

Mrs. Hoffman's room was exactly the same as Mr. Jones's except it had desks and chairs instead of science tables and stools. Harold left me at the door and Mrs. Hoffman welcomed me—I could see she'd been told I was coming—and pointed to a front desk near a window. I sat down and looked around. The kids in this room looked directly at the teacher when she was talking as if they were listening to everything she said. The boys didn't grease their hair back and they wore gym shoes instead of black pointed shoes. I noticed some Asian kids and some kids wearing glasses. It didn't surprise me to find myself here with them—I was always in the homeroom for the smartest kids—and I noticed I felt more comfortable here than I had in Mr. Jones's room. And I definitely felt more comfortable than I ever had at Cooley.

In my first week I could see different groups and I wondered which one I wanted to join. After school, on my first day at Blaine, I played touch football in the schoolyard. Paul Hernandez, a high school senior, was playing quarterback and he threw a lot of passes to me. In the huddle he told me to run deep pass patterns and I did and scored two touchdowns. Mike, Lee, and Ken Los were on the other team. Mike and Lee couldn't guard me because I ran faster than they did. Ken, another high school senior, got mad after I caught two touchdown passes and decided to guard me so I wouldn't catch anymore and then after that I didn't. I felt good about making a senior in high school guard me.

When the game was over I looked around the schoolyard. Harold and his friends were sitting on the short pillars that lined the field, smoking. Small kids were playing on the swings and slide. Some girls were walking around the playground and talking. Cars passed by on Southport Street. Everybody seemed to be paired off or in groups and I wanted to be part of a group myself but I didn't know which one. Joining a gang never crossed my mind and I wasn't a book worm. Sports, friends, and girls were at the top of my list of what I liked.

The next day I saw something that helped me make up my mind about what group I wanted to be part of. That day, in the schoolyard after school, two eighth-graders in my new homeroom, Larry and Lee, were hanging out by swings. Mike went up to them and started yelling good-natured taunts at them; he'd say something and run a little way away, then run back up to them and something else. Larry chased Mike down, tackled him, grabbed his shoe and threw it to Lee. Mike ran back and forth between Lee to Larry trying to get his shoe. All three of them were laughing and I could see Mike didn't mind. Eventually Lee gave Mike back his shoe and I thought the game was over. Then Larry looked at me and came after me. I could have gotten away if I had wanted to but I played along and let him catch me, get me down on the ground, and take off my shoe. Lee and Larry threw my shoe around a couple of times, but I didn't like chasing around after them like a little kid on a playground. So the third time they threw my shoe I grabbed it and took off running. They couldn't catch me and they gave up after we'd run about twenty yards. I stood next to the basketball court and watched them saunter back to the swings. That was the moment when I started to think of myself as less like Mike and more like Lee and Larry. Mike was friendly and smart. He played sports all the time but he didn't run very fast and he dropped a lot of football passes. He wasn't interested in girls. Lee and Larry and were good at sports, especially football, and they liked girls and girls liked them. Lee had two older brothers who went to Lake View High School and were both captains of the football team in different years.

Nothing happened that day or the day after that or even in the next few weeks that grew out of my decision to hang out with Lee and Larry more. But I knew who I was and who I wanted to be. Lee and Larry's friends became my friends and eventually Mike and Lee became my best friends. On Saturdays he stopped by my house, I went downstairs and knocked on Mike's door, and the three of us walked over to the schoolyard to play football. We played tackle football in the snow in the winter, touch football in the fall. I was always one of the first ones to be picked. Mike was always one of the last ones to be picked but he didn't mind. He just wanted to play.

I graduated from eighth grade from Blaine School in June 1968 and the next fall enrolled at Lane Technical High School as a freshman. You had to have good grades and get good scores on reading and math tests to get into Lane. It was a big high school of five thousand boys on a campus like that of a small college.

Chapter 12

Not One Play

Barack Obama says in his memoir, *Audacity of Hope*, that every man is either trying to live up to his father's expectations or make up for his father's mistakes. When I look back on my life in the late 1960s and early 1970s, when I was in high school, I can see that I was trying to make up for my father's mistakes. My father never had a job; I had been working since the age of eleven when I started my job at the polo ranch. My parents never told me to get a job. I did it all on my own, and when I think about it now I realize I probably wanted to be different from my father. Plus, I needed the money.

In 1971, when I was a junior in high school, I worked fifteen hours a week during the school year and full time in the summer in the Jack B Nimble candle shop in Chicago's Old Town. I liked having a part-time job. It put money in my pocket and gave me something to do after school when football practice ended. The candle shop was in Old Town, a cool section of town that attracted hippies. My oldest sister Aiko worked in Old Town as a glassblower and she got me the job at the candle shop. On Saturdays I cleaned and stocked the shelves with candles and incense before customers poured in starting at around four. The Richard Nixon and the red-white-and-blue dollar-sign candles were the big sellers. On Saturdays, after stocking the shelves, I stood on the shop floor helping customers and watching for shoplifters. I got paid to watch people. On occasion I had to ask a customer to put out a cigarette since smoking was not allowed in the shop. I helped customers find candles, but I never caught anyone shoplifting.

During the week I went to football practice. I was a second-string halfback on the varsity high school team—because I was second string I spent all my time on the bench, waiting to play. I wondered why I stayed on the team since I never got to play, not even once. Some the other guys on the second string got to play in conference games but somehow I and my good friend Rich never got in. I wondered what my father would say if I quit.

I wasn't exactly worried that he would think less of me if I quit, but maybe his expectations did have some effect on me, although if they did I had no idea at the time, and I'm not sure that's true. But he was a star football player in college and the captain of his team. He played in every game and scored many touchdowns to the roaring applause of his fans. He broke his collarbone twice and played the whole season anyway, and the guys on the team gave him the nickname Chalky. I couldn't imagine any of that happening to Eddie but I knew it was all true. Those days lived in my father's memory as if they had happened yesterday, and they must have had more effect on me than I knew, because why else would I not want my father to know I was thinking of quitting my football team?

I thought about all that almost every day, when I was walking the two blocks from the bus stop to my apartment after practice. I went back and forth in my mind about staying on the team or quitting. I didn't like going to practice everyday after school until it got dark but If I quit I wouldn't have anything to do after school. Besides, I thought girls liked guys on a sports team. And what would I tell my father if I quit? Finally I decided if I quit I wouldn't tell him, like I hadn't told him when I tried out for the team to begin with, when I was a freshman. I didn't tell him that because I didn't tell him anything about my life, I talked to him as little as possible, but also maybe I didn't tell him because what if I didn't make it?

The try-out took place in the last period of the first Friday of my high school freshman year. I finished third in the fifty-yard race and the coach didn't pick me for the team. But I didn't give up. I had thought I would make the team, my friends in the neighborhood had thought I would make the team, and I decided to keep trying. That day, at the end of class, I hurried across the gym and asked the freshman football coach if I could still come to the practice. He said I could.

None of the freshmen who made it onto the team, including me, played in the games—we just practiced with the other freshmen every day, running laps, doing push-ups, practicing blocking and tackling. As a sophomore I played in every game as a defensive halfback on the sophomore team. At the beginning of the football season in my junior year, the head coach told me I would be a second-string halfback, which ended up meaning I sat on the bench during every single game.

My father never came to any of my games. But then one day I looked across the field and there he was, standing in the visitor's section, wearing his long dark wool overcoat, holding his cane. I stared at him long and hard. I couldn't believe my eyes. What the hell was he doing here?

"I think that's my father," I said to my friend Rich.

"Go say hi to him," Rich said, like there would never be a reason in the world not to.

"Nah," I said. I didn't offer any explanation. I was startled to see my father at the game, in fact anywhere outside the house. He never left the house and I liked it that way. I didn't really want to have him showing up, meeting my friends, getting involved in my business. You can leave the house, I silently addressed him. It's a free country. Just don't come near me.

The game ended and I followed the team to the locker room without another glance at my father. The next day, a Saturday in mid-November, I took the Clark Street bus to work in Old Town. I got off the bus at North Avenue and walked two blocks to the candle shop. The shop manager, Jim, a man in his forties who was upfront about being gay, was counting money in the cash register behind the counter. I had been working there since last summer and I knew what to do without asking. I proceeded to vacuum the floor and restock the shelves with candles. When the shop got busy I stopped cleaning and started watching the floor. After working six hours I took the bus home. That night my friends and I went to the Century Theater on Clark and Diversey and saw Guess Who's Coming to Dinner. The movie had been out for a few years by then but I had never seen it. I remember sitting there in the theater watching Sidney Poitier, a black actor playing a black man in love with a white woman in an era when interracial marriage was so charged because of racial prejudice it wasn't even legal. I admired Sidney Poitier and the character he played in the movie, an accomplished doctor who had the courage to ask his white girlfriend's parents for her hand in marriage. For me it was less about racial politics and more about not letting things get in your way.

When I got home from the movies I went upstairs to my bedroom. My father had to pass through my room to get to his but I knew he would already be in bed and I wouldn't have to see him. But then, just before I jumped into bed, he yelled out to me, "Did you see me at your game?"

I walked into his room and looked at him lying on his cot against the far wall, wondering what I would say. I took a deep breath. "I saw you."

"You have a good team. How many guys are on it?"

"About eighty." I didn't want to talk. I wasn't used to talking with my father about my life. My interactions with him were always negative, him yelling at me for something I did. He read the newspaper sports section every day and I played sports anytime I could, but we never even talked about the Cubs or the Bears.

"I don't understand why the coach didn't put you in the game. Your team had a twenty- point lead."

"I don't get it either," I said, wanting to go to bed. I didn't feel bad about not playing in the game; I was starting to get used to it. It was my father who seemed to feel bad about it now and he wouldn't stop talking about it.

"It's your team," he said. "I hope you get to play."

"Thanks," I said. I went back to my room, feeling unexpectedly happy about talking to my father about something that mattered to me and surprised to be supported by him and a little uncomfortable, a little bit uneasy, all at the same time.

In the end I didn't quit the team even though I never got to play in my junior year. I liked the idea of being on the team and I didn't want to be thought of as a quitter like I thought of my father as a quitter. The next October, in the middle of my senior year football season, I was moved up to the first string. One day, during practice, when the third-string halfback was absent, I had to take his place to run against the first string defense so they could practice. I ran down the field, through and past the defense and nobody could tackle me. It happened over and over during a twenty-minute period. If it had been a real game I would have scored seven or eight fifty-yard touchdown runs. In practice the next day the coach put me on the first string offense and the kick-off return. And after that I played first-string halfback in every game. I ran a kick-off return to the fifty-yard line, caught a twenty-five yard pass, and scored in a play-off game.

"How long have you been playing?" my father called out from his room the day after the play-off game I scored in. It was early evening, the first week in November, and I was in my room getting ready to go into the kitchen for dinner. I'd never told my father I made it onto the first string. "Why didn't you tell me?" he yelled now. I could hear anger in his voice.

I didn't know what to say. I stood there trying to figure out how to answer that question.

"How did you score?" my father yelled, still upset. He was talking about the two points I made in the last game.

I walked into his room. "It was an extra point. A three-yard run."

He put the newspaper down and glared at me.

"How long have you been playing?" he repeated.

"The coach put me on the first string in October."

"Good for you. And you've been playing ever since?"

"Yeah."

"Why you... I would have gone to your games. Why didn't you tell me? I would have liked to see you play." He looked at me, and although he was upset, I could see he understood why I didn't tell him. My relationship with him had changed from when I was a little kid. He stopped hitting me around sixth grade. And now, in high school, I was almost as big as he was; he was six feet tall and weighed 200 pounds and I was five-foot-ten and 165 pounds. My days of getting hit by him with a board were over.

I looked down at the floor feeling uncomfortable and a little guilty. Wordlessly, I shuffled out of his room and into the kitchen.

My father never said anything more to me about my football playing. But it turned out it was still on his mind.

Chapter 13

The Scholarship

"Coach wants to see you," Lou said with a smile as we passed each other in the hall. Lou was the quarterback and captain of the high school football team.

"What's up?"

"You'll find out. You'll like it."

Why would the coach want to see me, I wondered. The football season had ended a month ago and I'd turned in my equipment.

The football office was near my locker and I hurried there at the end of the day.

Coach Brunswick was standing in the hall outside the office door.

"Lou said you wanted to see me," I said a little tensely, not quite believing I wasn't in trouble even though Lou said I wasn't.

"You got a letter from Illinois Wesleyan University," the coach said. "They want you to play football. Way to go, Prosise. Here you go. Take it home and show your parents. You've really come on."

I stood there in disbelief. I was a senior at Lane Tech, a public high school in Chicago with selected enrollment—you had to get good grades and do well on their entrance exams to get in. It was located on the corner of Addison and Western, a huge rambling red-brick building surrounded by a wide green lawn—it looked like a small college. It was attended by 5000 boys and this year, for the first time, 550 girls enrolled. I'd played football all four years I'd been here and this year I'd started playing on the first-string varsity team as a halfback in the middle of the season. I was pretty good but I'd never expected to play in college on a scholarship. In fact, in my junior year I almost quit because I didn't play in any of the games, I stood on the sideline during the games.

"Wow. Thanks, coach," I said. "Now what?"

"Talk to your parents. If you're interested, contact the coach at the university. Read the letter. It tells you what to do." Coach Brunswick told me.

I walked the two blocks home from the bus stop thinking about playing football at Illinois Wesleyan University. I knew I'd have to talk to my father about this. He'd always had a manual typewriter, a small black used Smith Corona with worn white keys, and he spent a lot of time in his room laboriously typing letters, hunting and pecking, to various people. When I was a sophomore he sent a letter to the Chicago Tribune and signed me up for the Fun Club, sponsored by the Tribune. I got free tickets to a football game—the NFL champions versus the college All Stars—at Soldier Field. Sitting under the lights with my friends among 50,00 fans watching a football game, the skies opened up and it poured like never before. The winds blew the rain sideways which hindered visibility. The game was called before it was over because all the fans including me and my friends ran out onto the field and slid around in the wet grass in the pouring rain. I'll always remember that game and sliding on the field.

I never thought I would have a chance to play football in college. I thought college football was for the stars on the team, not for guys like me who played second string for half the season. I had a feeling this scholarship had something to do with those letters my father wrote. He'd been the captain of the football team at Illinois Wesleyan in 1929. When he came out of his room on those rare occasions, he'd stand in the kitchen and talk about corresponding with Fred Young, who had been on the team with him all those years ago and was now a successful businessman who had donated a lot of money to the school. I sat at the table with my sisters and finished my dinner. My father must've told Fred Young about me and Fred Young must've pulled some strings, I realized.

When I got home I went directly to my father's room. He was lying on his cot thumbing through a Time magazine. I waited by the door until he looked up at me

"I got a letter from the football coach at Illinois Wesleyan University," I said.

"You did? I'll be darned." he said, his eyes sparkling behind his black horn-rimmed glasses. "What did it say?"

"They want me to play football," I answered proudly.

He nodded cheerfully, looking proud of me and himself. "Sounds great to me. What are you going to do?"

"I don't know." I felt thrilled to be offered a scholarship but something in me wasn't sure. Illinois Wesleyan was a long way away. Two of my older siblings had gone to UIC—University of Illinois Chicago; my sister Phyllis was still there. I associated Illinois Wesleyan with my father and I still couldn't love or forgive him for the past, which made me less than enthusiastic about the school.

"Do you want to visit the campus?" my father asked.

"Yeah, sure."

"I'll contact my friend Fred Young. He should be able to arrange a campus visit. I hope it works out."

"Thanks," I said. I appreciate it." I did appreciate it and in a strange way the fact that my friends heard that I got a letter to play football at Illinois Wesleyan University made me feel special, almost as special as the day at practice when the defense couldn't tackle me and coach put me on the first string. I stood there for a moment and then turned around and retraced my steps to the kitchen. My mom was doing dishes at the sink.

"What's going on?" she asked me excitedly.

"I got a letter today from Illinois Wesleyan University. They're offering me a football scholarship." It wasn't technically a football scholarship. Since Illinois Wesleyan is a Division III school, they don't offer athletic scholarships, they provide assistance.

I told my mother I wasn't sure I wanted to go to a school in Bloomington, two hours away, and she said the scholarship was a good opportunity but she would leave it up to me.

I went outside. Mike was standing on the sidewalk by the front steps of the building. "Let's walk over to Southport Street," I said. We walked along the sidewalk side by side, Mike looking in all the windows and picking up pebbles and tossing them at parking meters and me staring straight ahead. We stopped at the Music Box and looked at scenes from the upcoming movies on posters in a glass case. "I got a letter today from Illinois Wesleyan University. They offered me a football scholarship."

"Really? That's great news," Mike said enthusiastically. "What are you going to do?"

"I'm not sure."

"Where is Illinois Wesleyan? How'd that happen? Have you ever been there?"

" My father was the captain of the football team there years ago. It's in Bloomington, about two hours south. I hope to visit soon."

"Sounds good." Mike said looking at me curiously.

A week later on an early Saturday morning, Fred Young met me at the Bloomington Greyhound bus station. We shook hands and I got into his black 1970 Chevy Impala. "I'm glad you could visit us. I think you'll like our school. Your dad and I had four great years here. He was a heck of an athlete." Mr. Young said. He smiled broadly at me. He was wearing a white shirt, a gray v-neck sweater, and a red bowtie. He had the same black horn-rimmed glasses my father wore.

"Terrific," I replied. "Thanks for picking me up and for show-ing me the college. My father told me you both played football."

Mr. Young drove to the campus and parked in a big mostly empty parking lot. We got out and walked around the campus. We passed two brick classroom buildings and a huge rambling granite dormitory. On our right, on the other side of the dormitory was a large two-story gray-brick building with glass doors. Above the front entrance, in big black letters, were the words "Fred Young Field House."

"Wow, Mr. Young," I said. "The fieldhouse is named after you. You must be proud."

Mr. Young smiled at me benignly and said nothing. He took me to the student cafeteria in a dorm beyond the field house. We pushed our trays along the lunch line, both of us choosing ham and cheese sandwiches and bowls of chicken noodle soup.

"I spoke with Coach Hester and he's looking forward to having you on the team," Mr. Young said with a smile when we were seated at a long table by the windows.

"Thank you. Do you think he'll want to see film from my high school games?" I asked hoping he would say yes to prolong my day of glory.

"I'll check with him but I don't think it'll be necessary, " Mr. Young said. "If you want to come to school here just tell your dad and we'll work things out. We'll get you set up in a dorm and introduce you to some of the guys on the team."

When lunch was over he drove me back to the bus station. On the two-hour ride home I stared out the window at the cornfields wondering why I was more excited about telling my friends about my college visit than I was about attending Illinois Wesleyan and playing football on their team. I loved sports and so did my father but I still avoided talking with him. He read the sports section in the Tribune everyday and talked about playing football at Illinois Wesleyan every chance he got. It was clear to me that he was living in the past and wasn't paying much attention to the reality of who he was in the present, but the unpleasant reality of the past and present was all I could see of him. I had never envisioned him as a football player. I thought of him as an old man who walked with a cane and never went anywhere. He never had a job and use to come home drunk at night. In my junior year when I broke my ankle at football practice he told me that his former teammates gave him the nickname Chalky because he broke his collarbone twice when he was playing football. I couldn't handle being Chalky's boy. Maybe if I had had a different relationship with him or if he had been a different person I would have played football in college. Maybe I would have had a different vision of being a football player at Illinois Wesleyan and gone for it.

When I met with my counselor about college, both of us were relieved when I told her I would go to UIC. If I'd decided on Illinois Wesleyan, it would have meant more work for both of us. I didn't really know why I wanted to go to college. It seemed like the thing to do after high school since my older siblings went and my father always talked about Illinois Wesleyan. I decided to go to UIC, but I wasn't looking forward to telling my father.

On Thursday after school I dragged myself through my room and stepped into the cage. My father was lying on his cot reading The Reader's Digest. He looked up at me and said, "What goes?"

"I've decided not to go to Illinois Wesleyan," I said before I lost my nerve.

He closed the magazine, tilted his head and gave me a long look, then said in a low voice, "Why? It's a good opportunity. Are you sure?"

"I don't want to play football anymore," I said firmly. "I'll go to UIC like Phyllis."

My father shrugged and looked down at his magazine. "Okay. I'm disappointed but it's your life."

"Thanks for your help," I said as I turned away. I glanced back at him on my way out the door. He was lying on his bed again, immersed in his Reader's Digest.

After graduating from Lane Tech High School, I went on to the University of Illinois Chicago UIC where I received a bachelor's degree in history and a minor in education. I lived at home and commuted for the first three years. In my fourth year when I did my student teaching at Pierce School, I shared an apartment with a friend in East Rogers Park on the north side of Chicago.

Part III
Mansions and Schools

Housing Projects, Mansions and Schools:

Chapter 14

A Taste of Hate

I was standing at the counter in the office at Taft High School, waiting for my substitute teaching assignment, when I saw two kids, one black and one white, standing by the secretary's desk behind the counter, their bodies just inches apart and their faces full of hatred. They bumped chests and clenched their fists. The secretary looked on helplessly.

It was my first day as a substitute teacher at Taft. I had been transferred here after a month-and-a-half stint as a regular substitute teacher at Harper High School, an all-black high school on the south side in Englewood. I went to the school every morning and they told me what class I'd be teaching that day.

I'd gotten a bachelor's degree in history six months ago and was taking education classes and working as a substitute in the Chicago schools until I got a teaching certificate and could get a regular job as a teacher. College had been a lot like high school. I lived at home with my parents and took the el and subway downtown to UIC until my senior year when I moved into an apartment with a friend in East Rogers Park, about a mile from the school where I was doing my student teaching. When I started college I didn't know what I wanted to do for a living. But, I'd learned that I liked working with kids. Ever since I graduated from high school I'd been a Sunday school teacher, basketball coach, and camp counselor for my church, and every time I saw a kid's face light up because of something I said or did it made me happy. So I decided to become a teacher.

I was successful as a substitute teacher at Harper High School, kids listened to me and for the most part sat at their desks and did their work, read their books and did the assignments I gave them. It felt normal to be back in a school where almost everybody was black. Then I got a notice in November that I was being reassigned to Taft High School a predominantly white high school on the far northwest side of Chicago.. And now today, I was suddenly at Taft. As part of the Chicago Public School's federally mandated desegregation plan, forty black students were bussed into Taft. Their first day was my first day. On my first day at Taft, I did what I always did, I went to the school office to find out my substitute teaching assignment. I was standing at the counter signing in when it appeared that behind the counter a black kid and a white kid were about to exchange blows.

Before even thinking about what I was doing I went behind the counter and stepped between the two boys who were facing off by the secretary. The secretary stood up helplessly and watched. I placed a forearm on each boy's chest and the boys stepped apart. A tall white man in a dark-blue suit came into the office, said sternly, "Come with me," and escorted the two boys into his office behind the counter. I went back to the front of the counter. As I stood there waiting again for my teaching assignment, I felt adrenaline pumping through me. I looked at the two secretaries in the office and thought about how helpless they seemed, and I wondered why I didn't feel helpless. I knew it must've had something to do with growing up in Cabrini-Green and not being afraid of black people.

At a staff meeting in the school auditorium the next morning, the Taft principal, Mr. Ozaki, urged his staff to get involved and help with the integration of black students. He said a substitute teacher had broken up a fight in the office and used that as a positive example. I knew he was talking about me but nobody else did and I felt obscurely proud.

Mr. Ozaki introduced Joseph Hannon, superintendent of the Chicago Public Schools. Dr. Hannon stood at the podium in his dark-gray suit and tie and gave a speech. "Change is challenging," he said, but he also said, addressing Taft's staff, "This is not your school. This school belongs to the citizens of Chicago. Those kids will continue to be bussed here and they belong in this school too."

I looked around at the other teachers in the auditorium. At least half of them looked tense and worried about having a handful of black kids attending their school.

I wondered about their experience with black people, whether they'd had any and what it was. I'd grown up playing with black kids, going to school with them and being friends with them and I'd enjoyed working with them at Harper High School. It pained me to think of this handful of black kids being brought here and forced to attend school in a hostile environment. With all my heart I wished that they would be accepted. And even though I'd just been mentioned as a good example by the principal in front of the whole school, I felt skeptical about teaching at Taft. I'd never been around racism against black people and I knew I didn't want to be.

I was a substitute teacher at Taft High School for two months. The African American students sat quietly in class and answered the questions in the books, but schoolwork was secondary to the race issue. Tension filled the classrooms.

As well as racism, my time at Taft High School gave me a firsthand view of the changing demographics of Chicago and the effects of that on the schools. Chicago had always had a higher degree of residential black segregation than any other large northern city. Even so, neighborhood elementary schools used to be places that helped bring people from diverse backgrounds together. But by 1977, when I was a substitute teacher at Taft, the white portion of the Chicago school population had fallen by 75 percent due to "white flight" —white families moving to the suburbs, a trend that started in the 1950s and accelerated in the 60s and 70s; between 1960 and 1980 the white population in Englewood, currently the most racially polarized neighborhood in Chicago, fell from 51,583 to 518. Segregation was also promoted by the law. As early as 1910 and as late as 1950, African-Americans were denied federally backed loans to buy houses in racially mixed or white neighborhoods. In addition, many white students went to private schools. As a result, the student population in Chicago had become largely black and Hispanic. Taft was located in Chicago but it was on the far northwest side of the city that had remained a stronghold of white families, many of whom couldn't move to the suburbs because they worked for the city. The legal desegregation of the schools was mandated in 1976 by the Illinois State Board of Education and Taft was one of the first schools where black kids were bused in.

During the six months I was at Taft, the police were called to the school three or four times to break-up fights between the white kids and the black kids, and on two occasions the cops took some kids away in their car. I heard in the teachers' lounge that the boys had been fighting in history class—that was the first incident. I didn't hear anything about the second incident but I'm pretty sure it involved fighting too. When the cops came and picked up the kids, the students in my classroom rushed to the window to watch their classmates being taken away by the police. In the teachers' lounge a veteran Taft teacher told me I wasn't experiencing the real Taft. But it seemed to me that I was experiencing the real Taft—the Taft underneath the surface that usually stayed hidden until something—someone—came along: those forty black kids arriving on buses.

When I was transferred to a school in a different north side area, one that had poverty and gangs and crime, I breathed a sigh of relief. I didn't grow up around Hispanics, but I was comfortable around them because they were a minority and I was comfortable around minorities. I wasn't comfortable around racism.

Chapter 15

Statistics

It was a Wednesday morning in the week after spring break and I was standing in front of my classroom at Tuley Middle School. When I moved from Taft to Tuley I was hired as a regular teacher. At that time, 1977, it was common in public middle schools in Chicago to group kids in different grades together according to their reading ability. Last year, my first year at Tuley, I had sixth, seventh, and eighth graders in my classroom, all thirty-three of them deemed second from the top.

This year I was teaching eighth-graders in Chicago's Access to Excellence program, a program for students who were at risk of not graduating. There were only fifteen kids in my class and none of them would have ordinarily attended Tuley. They were all bussed in from other neighborhoods; Tuley had been designated a school where Access to Excellence was offered. All of my students had bad records, most of them had histories of behavior problems, and they all struggled academically.

I looked around the room at them sitting or slouching at their desks, looking back at me or looking out the window or staring down at their desks. I introduced the story they had to read that day, a story about a boy who wanted to play on the school basketball team and kept practicing until he made it. The kids opened their books and I circulated around the room looking at each of them as I talked more about the story. Everyone except Billy King, a tall coffee-colored thirteen-year-old from West Humboldt Park, was reading the story. Billy had been fiddling around at his desk, staring out the window, talking out loud to the kid next to him, for the last two days. I called his mother yesterday but didn't reach her. I wondered what had happened to him on spring break. I tried talking with him but I couldn't reach him either.

"When you finish reading the story, answer the first five questions and do the vocabulary section on page 125," I told everyone. "Any questions on what you're supposed to do?"

Willy rested his head on his right arm. I went over and stood next to him. "You know the rules, Billy," I said. "To be in my class you have to do your work. No sleeping. Get going. I don't want to have to keep telling you."

In the summer before I started teaching at Tuley I decided I was going to make my classes work by creating rules and consequences for breaking them. I remembered my seventh grade class at Cooley in Cabrini-Green where the kids sat around in class talking and reading comic books and the boys wandered out into the hallway without permission and spent chunks of time out there slap-boxing. I knew I didn't want anything like that in my classroom. I picked two rules. The first rule was treat all people with respect. Anybody who broke that rule had to apologize the first time and then write two paragraphs if it recurred. The second rule was spend your time wisely. The consequence for not spending your time wisely could mean, a phone call home, lose your desk and stand in the back of the room, or be sent to the office. I announced my rules to my students on my first day at Tuley and on the first day of school this year. Both times I gave them a chance to talk about them and ask questions. Everybody agreed that they were fair rules.

For the most part my rules worked well and the kids followed them. I'd learned during my student teaching that establishing rules and consequences helped kids understand boundaries. Reviewing the rules made class routines clearer for kids. Rules and consequences helped build relationships between teachers and kids because they let the kids know the teacher was fair. Good relationships with students is vital. If a student sees that the teacher is fair and wants what's best for the kids, the kids will be much more apt to cooperate and behave.

I walked back to my desk, sat down, and looked across the room. Most of the kids were working. Willy's head was still on his desk. I felt frustrated. I didn't want to kick Billy out of class but I didn't have a choice. I'd tried to call Billy's mother on Monday after school but she didn't answer her phone and making him stand in the back of the classroom had no effect. Willy's attendance had been spotty all year and in the seven months he'd been in my class he'd missed quite a few assignments.

I walked back over to his desk. "Okay Billy. You know the rules. Since you refuse to work you have to go to the office and stay there until your mother comes to school." The other kids stopped reading and writing and watched me. They understood, I thought: A rule is a rule. He'd left me no choice.

"Take this note and give it to Mr. Molina in the office. Like I said, you can't come back to class until your mother comes to school."

Billy stood up and I handed him the note.

"I don't blame you, Billy," yelled Alfredo. "This story is about to put me to sleep too."

"Alright, Alfredo," I said. "If you don't quiet down you'll be going with him."

Alfredo always did his work and never put his head on his desk, but he talked too much and when the class descended the stairs from the third floor at the end of the day he often leaned back against the wall and slid instead of walking. I told kids to stop talking all the time— when I worked with individual kids at my desk I had to tell the other students who were working at their desks to stop talking, almost daily. Sometimes when kids disrupted the class with talking I sent letters home to their parents or told the kids to stand in the back of the room until they were ready to work and sometimes I just reprimanded them. Everyday was a struggle, but I knew that if I couldn't manage student behavior I wouldn't be able to keep a job as a regular teacher at Tuley, and so managing student behavior was a priority for me.

Billy left the classroom and headed for the office.

"Okay, back to work," I said. I walked to my desk and sat down, thinking about Billy. The office would call his mother and I figured I'd hear from her later that day or the next day.

But I didn't. After two days and still nothing from Billy's mother, and after being asked nicely by the assistant principal, Mr. Molina, I said I would let Billy back in my class as long as he would agree to do his work. Mr. Molina brought him to my classroom and I told Billy in the hallway, while Mr. Molina was standing there, that he would have to do his work and there would no more sleeping in class. Willy nodded, looking down at the floor.

After that Billy did everything the other kids in my class did. When it was time to read a story, Billy was one of the first to open his book and look at me and he never put his head on his desk again. He seemed grateful that I had let him back in class and embarrassed that his mother hadn't come to school to talk to me. Every time I looked at him I wondered where his mother was and what she was doing, whether she worked more than one job or had some other worse problems, and I wondered if Billy ever saw his father because he never mentioned him in class. And ever since then I've wondered what happened to Billy himself, whether he was the one boy out of four who graduated from high school or whether he became some other kind of statistic, whether he was one of the other three, the ones who get killed in a shooting or end up in prison.

Chapter 16

No Police Report

It was the end of the school day and I had just dismissed my class. I was approaching the end of my third school year at Tuley. This year I had twenty-five sixth-, seventh-, and eighth-graders, kids with the lowest test scores. I was happy to have this low-scoring group. Most of them behaved and wanted to learn.

When one of the girls in my class, Cheryl, ran for student council president, she spent hours after school making her own posters and sometimes she made them during class when she was finished with her other work; I saw her laboring over them. The letters came out crooked and she didn't want to put the posters up in the halls. One day as I was in the hallway heading for my next classroom, I saw the counselor, Mrs. Smith, helping a girl from the high-achieving group, Sandra, who was running against Cheryl, put her posters up on a bulletin board. It came clear to me in that moment that Cheryl wasn't getting fair treatment and the reason she wasn't was that she was in the low-scoring group. At lunchtime I confronted Mrs. Smith in the student cafeteria about why she wasn't helping Cheryl. The kids in my class saw me do that and loved having their teacher stick up for one of them. That afternoon they sat up in their chairs and smiled and ever since they've been more interested in doing the work. And Mrs. Smith helped Cheryl put up her posters. Sandra won the election, but Cheryl got ten votes and after that she started getting better grades.

Today, once all the kids were gone, I strolled over to the windows and looked out. It was a warm spring day and a breeze was coming through the open window. On the sidewalk, three-stories below, I saw a hefty Hispanic teenage boy standing alone holding a brown paper grocery bag. He was a high school kid, too old to go to Tuley. Clusters of Tuley students were passing him on the sidewalk, going home.

As I watched, one of the school's security guards, Miguel Ortiz, approached the boy who was holding the bag. Miguel had grown up in the neighborhood and still lived here. He was my age, twenty-three, and was married and had a little boy. I played in pick-up basketball games with him after school twice a week and we were friends, and his two younger brothers went to the school; one of them was in my class.

Miguel was enforcing a school rule designed to prevent gang recruitment—no one from outside of Tuley was allowed on the school grounds before four p.m. "You can't be here," I heard Miguel say when he got within twenty yards of the teenager. Later on I found out that Miguel knew that the kid was there to recruit seventh and eighth-graders into the Latin Kings. Nobody ever found out why he had a machete with him.

The boy pulled a machete out of his brown paper bag and started walking toward Miguel. Miguel quickly back-peddled toward the school. Without breaking his stride he bent down and picked up a bottle that was sitting on the curb and fake-threw it at the teenager. The teenager slowed down but he didn't stop following Miguel.

When Miguel was five yards in front of the school door, he threw the bottle and darted into the school. I was relieved that he had gotten away. I had heard about gangs but I had never witnessed gang activity.

I ran down three flights of stairs to the administrative hallway. Two Chicago police officers were standing outside the school office with Miguel, one holding a clipboard, the other resting his hand on his gun in its holster. A little group of teachers had gathered in the hall and I joined them. The cop was asking Miguel standard questions to begin filling out his police report. What's your name, where do you live, and so forth. Miguel wouldn't answer any of them. Instead, every time the cop asked him a question he said, "That's okay, I'll take care of it." This exchange went on for fifteen minutes. Finally the officer said, "I can't believe you people," and he and his partner stormed off.

Miguel looked around and waved at us, said, "Thanks, people," and walked into the school office. I stood in the hall, stunned by what I had seen and by the fact that Miguel refused to file a police report. I walked back up to my classroom on the third floor thinking I had just witnessed street justice. I learned the next day that Miguel and his brothers and uncles met the gang-banger—the teenager who'd come to the school—and his gang in an alley that night and Miguel and the young guy fought it out with their fists.

Miguel never said anything to me about it, during our basketball games or otherwise, but after that I looked at him a little differently, with new respect and a little bit of fear.

When I lived in Cabrini-Green in the 1960's, the gangs were the Vice Lords and the Disciples. The gangs in Lake View were the Simon City Royals and the Latin Kings. I remember the Latin Kings at Tuley in the Humboldt Park neighborhood. In Cabrini-Green I didn't see any gang activity but I did see a man stumble down the street after being stabbed. When my family moved into Lake View my new friends pointed out gang members in our walks around the neighborhood. When I was a teacher Tuley, the Latin Kings had a presence. For the kids in my class at Tuley, gunfire was not uncommon.

Street gangs in Chicago emerged in the 1960's. The Black P-Stone nation evolved into a criminal organization whose members were involved in the drug trade and other criminal activities, such as robbery and murder. The crimes led to the incarceration of more and more young black men. In prison, gangs continued to thrive. Two distinct gangs were created, the People Nation and the Folk nation. Affiliate gangs formed under each nation, the Vice Lords and Latin Kings under people, and the Simon City Royals and Disciples under Folk. The rival gangs fought over turf and the drug trade.

Kids join gangs for a variety of reasons. In some neighbor-hoods in Chicago, such as East Rogers Park and Englewood, gang membership is a given. Gangs provide kids with a sense of belonging, protection, and a way to make money.

To this day, people are shot daily in the streets of Chicago, particularly in the African American neighborhoods in the south and west sides. Gangs are a big part of the problem. The lack of trust and cooperation between the community and the Chicago Police Department contributes to the problem of violence.

Chapter 17

Have You Two Met?

I jogged onto the court, picked up a basketball, and dribbled around.

My wife and I had been going regularly to Edgewater Baptist Church, in the Edgewater neighborhood on the north side, for two years. Six months in, Mike Swanson, the coach of the church basketball team, recruited me to play with them.

After teaching at Tuley for three years I'd decided, at the age of 25, that I loved teaching but I didn't want to do it for the rest of my work life. A few years earlier I'd been the director of the summer camp I'd gone to when I was a kid, Camp Lake Chi Co, and I liked working with the counselors organizing programs and doing other administrative duties. So I decided to become a principal. I got a full-time, low-paying, entry-level administrative job at Loyola University and became a part-time Ph.D. student there, a part-time janitor in an apartment building for reduction in rent, and a new dad.

I'd met my wife, Ellen, when I was 23 and teaching at Tuley. We met at a church supper at the church I'd gone to since I was a kid; Ellen was there with a friend. I called her afterwards and asked her out to dinner. Over plates of lasagne at Papa Milanos, we learned we had been both camp counselors. She was a senior at University of Illinois and was planning to become a teacher. We got married after dating for a year. Ellen taught in Waukegan, a suburb forty-five minutes north of Chicago, until our first child, Lauren, was born. After that we moved into a drafty third-floor two-bedroom apartment in my sister Aiko's apartment building in

Lake View. As a way to get a $50 reduction in our monthly rent of $150, I had to vacuum the stairs in the building year round and shovel snow in the winter.

"Have you two met?" Mike, the coach, looked at me and pointed to an African-American man who had dark skin, was six feet tall, and probably weighed over 200 pounds.

I dribbled toward the guy and we shook hands. "I'm Roger," I said.

"I'm Mickey. Good to meet you. You been on the team long?"

It was fall, the beginning of basketball season. "This'll be my second year." This was Mickey's first time playing on the team. I had never seen him before although later I started running into him at church.

The coach walked off the court to talk on his phone. Mickey and I shot baskets as we waited for the other players to show up. Mickey grabbed a rebound and stuffed it, then dribbled the ball twenty feet from the basket, turned around and swished the shot.

I took a shot fifteen feet away from the basket. It went in so I kept shooting.

"Did you play college ball?" I asked Mickey. We continued to take turns shooting.

"Yeah. At North Dakota State a Division 3 school in North Dakota. I've got a couple of friends coming tonight who played college ball. We should have a nice squad."

"How'd you like North Dakota?"

"I loved it. I was in a small town and there wasn't much to do. But I met my wife Luanna there. You'll meet Roe and Ron tonight. Ron played at North Dakota with me and Roe played with me in high school at Cooley."

I stopped dribbling and looked at him. "You played at Cooley?"

"Yeah," Mickey said.

I wondered if he had been at Cooley when I was. I couldn't remember seeing him in the halls there. He'd said he'd played on the high school team but he looked younger than I was, so he was playing basketball after I'd left. What's he going to say when I tell him I went to Cooley, I thought. I pictured his surprise when he found out that I, a white guy, had gone there, a school in Cabrini-Green.

His friends Ron and Roe walked in and set their gym bags with the others by the bleachers across the gym.

"Take your sweats off and get out here," Mickey yelled.

"It smells like an old gym shoe in here," Ron hollered back.

Mickey and I kept shooting. "What position did you play at Cooley?" I asked him.

"I was a forward all four years," he said, shooting a ball from the free throw line.

I looked over at his friends. One was 6'4" and one was my height, about 5'10".

"How did your team do?"

"We did alright. Lost to Crane in the quarter-finals."

I took a breath. "I went to Cooley for seventh grade," I said. I looked at Mickey to see his response.

"No way," said Mickey, widening his eyes and gaping at me.

"I did. I went to Jenner through sixth grade and then Cooley for seventh."

"I don't believe you," Mickey said. He passed the ball to me. "Nobody like you went to Cooley."

I wasn't surprised he didn't believe me. My friends in Lake View when I first moved there had a hard time believing I'd lived in Cabrini-Green too. Sometimes I didn't believe it myself. I was white—Asian-American—and everybody in Cabrini was black. But I did live there, and it had partly made me who I was.

I took a shot. "I lived in the rowhouses till my second month of eighth grade. At Cooley I had Gymsky for homeroom, Erickson for English, and Mr. Thompson for PE."

I stared hard at Mickey to see how he would react. I liked knowing we had a connection. I could see that he was a nice guy and a really good basketball player and I wanted him to want to be friends with me. But I wasn't sure whether I was a good enough basketball player to measure up to his standards, and I couldn't tell how he felt about me saying I had lived in Cabrini. Did he really think I was lying? Or even bragging?

Mickey just looked at me for a few more seconds as if he was thinking about what I'd said. Then he grinned, dribbled the ball hard on the floor, jumped three feet in the air, and sank a twenty-foot shot. "I guess you did go to Cooley. Fooled me," he said. "How'd you survive?"

I opened my mouth, thinking about how to answer that question. Then Ron and Roe ran onto the court and started dribbling and shooting the ball.

"About time," Mickey yelled at them.

"Once we get a few more guys here we'll start layup lines," yelled Mike the coach from the sideline.

When practice started we did layup lines and practiced free throws before playing pick- up games for the rest of the night. We played until nine o'clock, then Mike said, "Let's wrap it up. I've got to work tomorrow."

I threw Mike his basketball and sat on the bleachers next to Mickey. As we pulled our sweatpants over our gym shorts, Mickey told me he was a caseworker for the Christopher House, a special education facility on the north side. I told him I worked at Loyola as the assistant to the dean. It turned out Mickey lived in an apartment building near my church and he invited his friends to church. After that night he and I became friends. We played basketball together twice a week. We shook hands and talked about sports whenever we ran into each other at church. I loved basketball and it felt good to play on a team, especially after working all day at Loyola and going to grad school two nights a week. We didn't have much time to socialize outside of basketball and church, but we were still friends.

That night, the night we met, as we were heading out the door together to go home, I thought again about Mickey's question:

How did you survive in Cabrini-Green? And then the answer came to me: I survived through my friendships. I kept to myself and didn't look for trouble but I always had friends. I would have gotten beaten up more than once if my friend Lorenzo hadn't stood up for me. I didn't fit in, but I fit in with my friends who did.

Everything was different in my life now, but in a way it wasn't that different. I still wanted to fit in and I still had friends who did fit in.

Chapter 18

Parents

I walked into Mrs. Ingram's fourth-grade classroom at Washington School and said, "Hi. I'm Roger Prosise the assistant principal. Thanks for coming in."

Mrs. Ingram and Mr. Jones, a tall white man in khakis and a short-sleeve shirt, were sitting in student chairs in a corner in the back of the room. Mr. Jones stood up and shook my hand. "Hi. I'm Mr. Jones, an ex-marine and a taekwondo instructor," he said.

I pulled out a chair and sat down, wondering what kind of meeting this would be.

"My wife couldn't make it," Mr. Jones said. "I know you talked with her on the phone and you know we don't agree with your decision." Mrs. Jones wanted her daughter to have Mrs. Jennings as her teacher and was disappointed I wouldn't move her out of Mrs. Ingram's classroom. I had invited Mrs. Jones to come and meet Mrs. Ingram for reassurance, but instead she'd sent her husband.

It was nine o'clock in the morning now on the Friday before the first day of school. It was my second year as assistant principal at Washington. When I was assistant to the dean at Loyola, back in 1983, I thought about pursuing a career at a university, either teaching as an administrator, but I decided to pursue a job as an administrator in a public elementary school. My teachers at Jenner in Cabrini-Green had made a huge difference in my ability to get along there. Now, I thought, I might be able to make a similar difference in some kid's life, not as a teacher—I'd already done that and wanted to try something new, but as someone who made decisions that could help young people succeed in school.

Dr. Heller, chairman of the department of educational leadership at Loyola, had connections with many of the suburban school districts in the Chicago area. He knew the superintendent for Washington's district and helped get me the interview to be the assistant principal here. Washington was in Libertyville, an upper middle-class suburb about twenty-five miles north of Chicago. By then my wife and I and Lauren, who was five, were living in a townhouse in West Rogers Park, a middle-class neighborhood in the northwest part of Chicago.

I looked at Mrs. Ingram and Mr. Jones. Mrs. Ingram, a veteran teacher with brown hair and glasses who kept to herself, was a good teacher but she wasn't popular with the kids and their parents. Mrs. Jennings was popular; she was easy going and had a sense of humor and everybody liked her. She was a good teacher too, but Mr. Jones' daughter wouldn't thrive any more in her classroom than she would in Mrs. Ingram's. In any case, Mrs. Jennings' room was full and we couldn't move Emily there.

Mrs. Ingram reviewed the fourth-grade curriculum and the makeup of the class for Mr. Jones. "We have 24 kids in the class and 13 of them are girls. In the morning I teach language arts. I meet with students in groups based on their learning needs. We generally have math in the afternoon."

Mr. Jones listened. Then he said somberly, "Have you ever had a little person in your class?"

Mrs. Jones had referred to her daughter during our phone call as a little person. "Do you know what a little person is?" she said to me then.

"Aren't all fourth-graders little people?" I said.

"No," said Mrs. Jones. "A little person is a midget. My daughter has a medical condition that prevents her from getting taller than a young child."

"I didn't know that about Emily. But the kids at our school are wonderful and I'm sure Emily will have no problems making friends and fitting in."

"No I have not," said Mrs. Ingram. "But the kids in my class are wonderful and I'm sure your daughter will have no problem making friends."

I looked at Mrs. Ingram now and thought that her response to Mr. Jones had been great.

Looking at me, Mr. Jones said angrily, "You won't make the change?"

I said that I agreed with Mrs. Ingram. "Your daughter will be fine."

"I hope you're right. I don't want to go to the board," Mr. Jones said.

He stood up and Mrs. Ingram and I followed suit. Mrs. Ingram shook his hand and said, "I'm glad we met. Feel free to visit anytime."

"Call me if you ever have a concern or question," I said shaking his hand.

"I will," Mr. Jones said scowling.

Once he was gone Mrs. Ingram looked at me and said, "I've been teaching for fifteen years and that was the most intense parent conference I've ever had. I see you drew the short straw. Where's Joe?" Joe was the principal at Washington. He'd told me to handle the meeting because he was busy and I had talked to Mrs. Jones on the phone.

"What was that about being a taekwondo instructor?" I said. It was clear that Mr. Jones was trying to intimidate me. Still, I was glad the principal had let me handle the meeting. I liked the challenge of working with difficult people. "You did a nice job with the meeting," I said to Mrs. Ingram. "I'm sure his daughter will be fine."

"I'll keep you posted," said Mrs. Ingram.

We walked out into the hall where teachers were putting up welcome-back-to-school posters. I walked to the main entrance and then went outside. It was a warm sunny late- August day.

I stood on the sidewalk looking at the green lawns and thought about the meeting with Mr. Jones. He was intense and wanted things his way. The parents weren't like this at Tuley, I thought.

I thought about Billy King, whose mom wouldn't come to school and who never saw his dad. It wasn't hard to see how Billy could drop out and end up in a gang. I didn't like the pressure from Mr. Jones. Mr. Jones seemed like he might have some problems of his own. But he was there for his kid, showing up, trying to make things better for her, and that was a good thing. I thought of Emily too. She might not fit in, I thought, but maybe that was less important than having parents who would go to bat for you. And then I thought about Billy's mother and father again and wondered who didn't go to bat for them and why they couldn't. The difference between a kid who graduates from high school and one who drops out is the presence or absence of a significant adult in that kid's life, rich or poor. I'd read that recently in an article written by Herb Wahlberg, an education researcher at UIC.

I never heard from Emily's parents again, and the few times I spoke with Mrs. Ingram she said Emily was doing just fine. She had made friends and had no trouble doing the work in class.

Chapter 19

More than Test Scores

I was sitting at a table with seven second-grade boys. I was the principal at Bell now. Bell was a small public grammar school located in Morton Grove, a middle-class suburb ten miles north of Chicago. We had 340 students, all in kindergarten through fourth grade. I took the job as principal here last year after being assistant principal at Washington for two years.

It's the middle of March and I've been having lunch every Wednesday with these particular boys for three months. We sit at the kidney-bean-shaped table in Mrs. Doherty's classroom for about twenty minutes, eat lunch, and talk, and then they go outside for recess. Six of these boys, Ryan, Scott, Kevin, David, Peter, and George, all of them friends, were picking fights with other kids on the playground. They also weren't finishing their school work or paying much attention in class. A teacher committee that suggested interventions for troubled students asked me to have lunch with the boys once a week to encourage them to behave and do their school work. The committee also decided to pick one other boy who wasn't fighting or struggling with his schoolwork, Robby Davis, to each lunch with us, thinking that he could be a good role model. Nobody told any of the boys why they were having lunch with me and I think they saw it as something fun that they wanted to do.

We opened our brown paper bags and took out our sandwiches. Most of the boys had peanut butter and jelly. I had a bologna sandwich and an apple. When we first started doing this I did most of the talking and the boys mostly only talked when I asked them questions about what books they were reading, whether they were getting much homework, how they were doing in class, what they did last weekend. Once I asked them what they watched on television and found out that six out of seven of them had TVs in their bedrooms. I thought about how my sisters and brothers and I watched TV together all the time when I was a kid and wondered how these boys having their own TVs in their rooms—a forerunner to kids having smart phones and iPads nowadays—affected them and their families.

Now, after all the lunches we've had together, the boys were talking more freely. They could leave when the bell rang for recess but they stayed and talked. The school committee's strategy worked: The boys had pretty much stopped fighting on the playground and were listening in class and doing their work. Even Robby seemed to be benefitting; he was more out-going than he was before and had six new friends. And it's something that the teachers asked me to continue.

Today, as soon as we started eating, David said his dad was going to buy him a puppy, a chocolate lab. All the other boys got excited by that and started talking about their dogs. I told them I had a dog when I was high school, a small cream-colored mutt named Taffy, but I didn't have a dog now. The bell rang, we all threw our trash away, and the boys dispersed, going to their lockers in the hall—all except Ryan, who stayed behind as if he wanted to tell me something. I waited for him to say what he wanted. We stood there looking at each other silently. I was tempted to prompt him but it seemed better to let him take his own time. Finally he swallowed hard and said, "My parents are getting a divorce. My dad moved out over the last week."

I was stunned. This was 1989, and although divorce had become a lot more common since the 1970s with the help of no-fault divorce laws—as I write this in 2016, about a million children per year have seen their parents divorce since 1974—Ryan was the first child who'd ever told me his parents were getting divorced. In fact, I'd never had a child tell me anything deeply personal about his home life. "How are you taking it?" I asked.

Ryan stared back at me teary eyed and said, "I'm okay." He lowered his head and started sobbing quietly.

I put my hand on his shoulder and said, "Things are going to work out." But standing there looking at his dark brown hair, at the cowlick standing up at the top of his head, I wasn't so sure about that. But I was glad I was there.

The next morning Ryan's mom came to school, sat with me in my office, and cried. She said that last night Ryan had told her that he told me about the divorce. "As far as I know it's the only time he's ever talked to anyone about it," she said. "He's never said anything about it at home. I've been wondering how he was taking it. Thanks so much for being there for him."

I could see that Ryan wasn't taking it well at all but I didn't want to say that to his mom, who obviously felt bad enough already. So instead I just talked about my lunches with the boys and told her we would offer Ryan as much support as possible here at the school.

She talked and cried some more and I just listened. Finally she blew her nose and dried her eyes. "Okay. I'll let you get back to your work."

"I'm glad you came in. Good luck and let me know if I can do anything more."

We stood up and shook hands and she left the office just as the morning bell rang. I watched her walk away, feeling sad for her and Ryan but also glad that she'd come in to talk and glad that Ryan had felt he could talk to me. Ryan's problem reminded me that there's more to school than raising test scores.

In the years to come, I will see, as a principal and then as a superintendent, a lot more parents divorcing and a lot more kids being affected by divorce. And even though I'll understand that some people do need to divorce, that some divorces might even be better for the kids—that that might have even been the case with my own parents, when I was a kid we always wondered why my mother never left my father—it will never get easier to watch my students go through it.

Statistically, children of divorced parents are two to three times more likely to suffer from serious social or psychological problems than their peers from intact families. There were a lot of broken families in Cabrini-Green when I was growing up. I don't remember seeing any dads there except for my friends Milton and Phillip's fathers, and my own, of course. The combination of poverty and broken families is a formula for failure. But not all kids who face those challenges fail. The presence of a significant adult who supports them—someone who means something to them, a parent, a teacher, a coach, an uncle, a grandmother, staff members at a Boys or Girls Club— means a child is more likely to graduate from high school whether they're rich or poor.

I hoped Ryan's parents worked things out and stayed together, but there was no way to know whether that would happen. Once spring rolled around, there was no keeping the boys inside so our once-a-week-lunch group came to a sudden end. At first they ate lunch with me and then ran outside and joined the other kids on the playground instead of staying and talking to me. Then a few days later they stopped even eating lunch with me. "You can't compete with sunny weather," a veteran second grade teacher yelled across the hall as my seven boys ran past us. I understood how they felt. I wanted to go outside too but instead I made my way back to the office.

Chapter 20

Jumping In

I was driving west on Interstate 88 to the White Pines campground in Oregon, Illinois. White Pines was an hour away from East Prairie, the kindergarten through eighth grade school where I'd been principal for the last four years. East Prairie was in Skokie, a mostly middle-class suburb of Chicago with a high Jewish and Asian population as well as people from many other ethnic and cultural groups; we had kids from families that spoke fifty different languages and some kids from low-income populations. The diversity was a good fit for me.

At the end of every school year the sixth-grade class at East Prairie rode on two different buses with four teachers and two parents to camp and swim for a three-day 'outdoor education program' at White Pines. The sixth grade teachers had urged me to join them on the last day of the three-day program. I thought it would be good for the kids to see me out of school, and besides, I was relishing being out of the office on a warm sunny late Friday morning.

I cruised along in my black Mazda 626, listening to James Taylor sing Sweet Baby James on a cassette. I saw the White Pines exit sign and drove to the campground. I pulled into the lot and parked my car next to one of the yellow school buses. I stepped out of the car onto the white stone parking lot. From the lot, I could see and hear kids jumping and screaming in the pool beyond the office and gift shop. Ten or twelve kids were standing on the deck or sitting in chairs at round white, glass-topped tables by the edge of the pool.

"Hey, Dr. Prosise," yelled Amy, a sixth grader who was standing on the deck with a light orange towel wrapped around her hair.

"Where's everybody else?" I yelled back. "How was the week?"

"They're over in the gift shop," she said.

I walked to the pool and saw Burt, one of the sixth grade teachers, standing with two students near the pool. "How'd it go out here?" I asked him.

"We got lucky with the weather, just like today, sunny and high 70s. I'm glad you came out. The kids are having a great time. We're giving them one last swim, then they're going to finish up their arts and crafts project. I'm jumping in one more time too. Why don't you join us in the pool? It feels great."

Should I jump in the water, I thought. I stood there in the sunshine in my purple shorts and white golf shirt and watched the kids and teachers splashing and laughing in the pool. I pulled off my shirt and dove in. I swam the width of the pool a few times, then got out, found a white towel and dried myself off and lay down on a chaise longue.

I closed my eyes and thought about my four years as principal at East Prairie. The kids were doing really well and had been since I started there. I was hired to work with the teachers on instructional issues. The previous principal had been mostly consumed by problems in the buildings and on the grounds. The school looked great but some of the students were struggling and the teachers wanted new programs. At the time the teachers had been hungry for a leader who would devote time to curriculum and staff development instead of things like leaking roofs—the superintendent had told me that when he hired me. In my previous job at Hynes I'd helped train teachers to use manipulatives—blocks and stuff like that—to teach math to kindergarten students through fourth graders. During my first year at East Prairie I'd led sessions in critical thinking skills in a new peer teaching program—a program where the teachers met once a month and took turns teaching each other how to be better teachers in whatever their specialties were. I also facilitated language arts curriculum development meetings with teachers, worked with teachers to raise academic standards for the sixth, seventh, and eighth grade students who were on the basketball, volleyball, and track teams, and led a parent committee that brought in new playground equipment. I also led a teacher committee that looked at how to improve student behavior; we came up with policies, such as contacting parents sooner when their kids were acting out, and developed consistent codes for student conduct. That year the writing scores in third grade at East Prairie were the tenth best in the state and the boys' basketball team won the conference championship. Since then the teachers and students have been learning and growing more every year. Test scores continue to be high across the board and I've been working with our teachers on some new middle school practices such as teaching teams—all the teachers in any given grade collaborating to help individual kids in whatever ways the kids need.

We've had struggles too. One year five or six parents of the kids in the gifted and talented program complained about the program and teacher, and the year before that the students and parents complained about the science teacher. They thought she was unfair and mean. At the end of the year, the science teacher retired and the gifted teacher resigned. Life is filled with struggles and at times failures, but the key to success is that when life knocks you down, you get up again. Fall down seven times stand up eight (Chinese proverb).

But for the most part it had been great working at East Prairie and even the hard parts were instructive to me. Even though I was their supervisor I was becoming friends with some of the teachers so I would miss them. Lying there by the pool I felt momentarily sad that I wouldn't be coming back to East Prairie next year. About two months ago the superintendent of a neighboring school district, John Cahill, contacted me about a superintendent job opening up in Bannockburn, a wealthy suburb about an hour north of Chicago. I'd known John Cahill for about four years. He did consulting for an executive educational search firm. I wasn't sure if I should apply for the job. I had never wanted to be a superintendent. I still enjoyed being a principal and my next career move was to be a director of personnel in a large school district. A superintendent is the CEO of a school district; he's hired by the local board of education and he reports to them. Board members are elected and as such may have agendas that may not necessarily align with promoting the best interests of the students and their education. I originally had some doubts about whether I wanted I wanted to be in that position. But after two unsuccessful interviews with boards of education in two middle class suburbs for two other superintendent positions I thought I might as well apply. I had nothing to lose and it was just an interview. Plus, every day I watched the superintendent of East Prairie do his job and it didn't seem that difficult. He'd never had a political run-in. He was going to be involved in a big scandal next year that would result in him losing his job—but that hadn't happened yet and at this point it looked like he was doing pretty well.

I had an interview for the job two months after I applied. I met Jim Warren, another consultant from the search firm, at the Doubletree Hotel. "I've heard you're a man of integrity," Jim Warren said as we shook hands. "John Cahill told me about you." John was the superintendent in the district next to East Prairie. He interviewed me for two other superintendent vacancies so this time he just listened. The two other vacancies were in middle class suburbs and even though I didn't get one, I wasn't going to stop trying.

I felt humbled and speechless. I'd read a lot about leadership and the importance of integrity but I'd never thought about whether I had integrity or what kind of impact I was having on my school.

Jim Warren asked me to tell him about myself and I talked about teaching at Tuley and what I learned from teaching in the inner city. I jumped over my years at Loyola University and talked about my years at Hynes and what I learned about hiring and training excellent teachers there.

As the sun beat down and my shorts dried out, I thought about Jim Warren saying he'd heard I was a man of integrity. It was true, I realized, and then I wondered where my integrity had come from. And I thought about power: What do you do with it and where do you get it? I hadn't said anything about growing up in Cabrini-Green during the interview, but now I thought about my experiences there. The people who lived in Cabrini didn't have power in the general society. They were poor and jobless, and some of them tried to get power by forming gangs. The gangs led to crime which led to prison or death. A black male in Cabrini had a twenty-five percent chance of graduating from high school. As a kid in Cabrini-Green, I felt powerless too.

As an adult, I had power as a principal. I had a say in who got hired and who got fired. I was the one who gave kids detentions when they had behavior problems. I made decisions to help kids succeed in school. At Bell I stood up to my boss, the superintendent, to defend a good teacher. That story and others like it must have leaked and led to the integrity comment. It's true that I was honest and treated people fairly. When someone with power has integrity, it helps pave the way to progress.

There's power in friendship too, I thought. When Mike, my new neighbor in eighth grade, reached out and became friends with me, he accepted me and therefore empowered me. My new friend made entering a new place less daunting. In fact, because of Mike, it was a breeze.

Having friends is one of the most important parts of going to school. Kids look forward to going to school to be with their friends. When I was a kid at Cooley in Cabrini-Green, those of my friends who were accepted by the older kids had power—they didn't get hassled. And they used that power to help other kids, like me—like Lorenzo standing up for me when gang members wanted to beat me up on our way back to school after lunch on my last day at Cooley. At Bannockburn, one of my goals as a superintendent would be to help every kid in the school district have at least one friend, I thought now, lying beside the pool. And I started to think about how I could make that happen. Integrity, power, and friendship, a potent combination, I thought.

After my interview, the consultant told me to drive by Bannockburn School and take a look. The following week I drove by Bannockburn School and noticed all the plush lawns and million dollar homes. Two of the homes even had horse corrals. I had an interview with the board of education during the first week in May. I sat at the end of a big glossy table with all seven members of the board of education in the library at Bannockburn School. I was wearing my dark blue suit, white shirt and red tie. I was comfortable and felt confident.

There were four women and three men and they all took turns asking me questions. The questions ranged from how I worked with teachers, communicated with parents, and disciplined students, to why I wanted to be the superintendent at Bannockburn. My experiences helped me answer their questions clearly and in detail. I knew I had been a successful principal at two schools, that I worked well with teachers and parents, and that I wanted what was best for all kids. I was the first of six candidates to interview for the job. After the first round of interviews with the board of education, two final candidates were asked back to meet with a group of Bannockburn teachers and a group of parents. These meetings didn't seem like interviews but rather simple conversations about the school. There was another interview with the board of education. At one point during that a board member asked me if I knew Michael Jordan's kid was going to be in kindergarten at Bannockburn School and I said I did. (Jim Warren had told me during my initial meeting about the job.)

"Why?" I said. "Is there some kind of special security I should be aware of?" The board seemed impressed that having Michael Jordan's kid in my school didn't awe me.

After that interview I became the top candidate, and then six out of seven board members spent the day at my school, meeting with groups of students, teachers, parents, administrators, and board members. At the end of the day, when the board members came out of their last meeting, with a group of students, one of the board members said to me, "We love your school and wish our school was like it." And then the president of the board grinned at me and said, joking, "If you and I can't work something out, which won't happen, we're going to offer the job to Eddie Chrystaudis" Eddie, the president of our student council, was one of seven students I'd picked to meet with the board. He was smart, likable, athletic, and out-going. I smiled, thinking about Eddie, feeling proud of him and the other kids who met with Bannockburn's board.

Last week, Jim Warren called and offered me the job. I asked about salary and benefits and then I accepted the offer. Whatever doubts I'd had about being superintendent had disappeared over the course of all those interviews, and I was excited about starting the job in July.

Burt, the sixth grade teacher, got out of the pool, came over, and touched my shoulder. "I'm heading over to the gift shop," he said. "Don't fall asleep in the sun. Get up and come with me."

I sat up and looked around. The pool was empty. The kids must've either gone back to their cabins to finish their craft projects or to the gift shop to buy stuff to bring home. I followed Burt into the little gift store. We wanted to be on the road by two o'clock so we could all get home in time for dinner.

Chapter 21

Mansions

It was a hot day in July 1994, my first day as the superintendent of Bannockburn School. Bannockburn was a one-school district, and I'd been hired to be not just the superintendent, but the principal and business manager as well. I'd known all along that I'd be the only administrator here; there had been a principal in previous years but the last one left at the same time as the previous superintendent and the board of education decided not to hire a new principal. This job was going to involve plenty of new territory for me: I'd be encountering new challenges as a superintendent and as a business manager. But working with an affluent community felt like it would be the biggest challenge for me. Even though I was a superintendent, in a way, I was still the kid who needed a scholarship to go to summer camp. I didn't think anybody would think less of me if they knew I grew up in poverty, but a part of me continued to worry about it. I felt like a pair of old jeans in a community of designer clothes.

I was wearing khakis and a short sleeved white shirt because it was summer and I knew very few people would be around today. It was eight in the morning and the board president, Dennis Levine wearing a short-sleeve red checkered shirt, was there to welcome me. He introduced me to Joan, the long-time secretary, wished me well, and left. I was armed with good intentions and had plans for getting off to a good start. One of those plans was to visit classrooms and talk to teachers and kids rather than just stay in my office and do paperwork. I sat at the desk in my new office. The office was surprisingly small and dingy, with an old wooden desk and a window air conditioner. It dawned on me that I wasn't given a tour of the school before the job offer was made and now I understood why. I reviewed the teaching assignments for the upcoming year, saw that there was a music teacher vacancy, and contacted local universities and the Regional Office of Education to post the music teacher vacancy. Then I decided to visit the summer school classroom. I walked down the carpeted hall to the first-grade classroom around the corner.

It was an old building with blue carpeted halls and lantern-shaped light fixtures hanging from the ceiling. The lanterns didn't give off much light so the hallway was dim. I was surprised by the poor condition of the building. The blue carpet was old and worn and there were battered brown wooden lockers for the kids in fourth grade. The younger kids hung their coats from hooks in the classrooms, Tuley School in the inner city was in better condition than Bannockburn, I thought. I entered the first grade classroom where summer school was being held. Mrs. Hayes was sitting with two boys at a round table and a couple of other kids were seated at desks. One of the boys was slowly reading from a copy of The Cat in the Hat while Mrs. Bentley listened patiently. I stood next to her desk for a minute and listened without interrupting when suddenly, without warning, a large white cork panel fell from the ceiling and crashed onto the empty desk next to me. Particles of dust settled and we all stared at each other like startled animals. I was stunned. Kids sitting at their desks jumped up. Then the teacher stood up and held out her hand to me.

"Welcome to Bannockburn School."

"What's this?" I asked her.

"This community has a lot of money but they don't spend it on the building. You'll see. Welcome. I'm Gen Hayes."

"Let me know if I can do anything to help with summer school," I said, thinking I might need more help than her.

I left the classroom and walked around the school before returning to the office. The classrooms were old with chalkboards and brown wooden desks bolted to the floor and kidney bean tables for small reading groups and a computer on a student desk near the teacher's desk. I walked down the hall to the custodian's office, wondering how such a rich community could have a school that looked so old and worn and seemed to be falling apart. I hope I don't have to spend much time on problems like this, I thought.

I found the head custodian sitting at his desk eating a salami sandwich. He was also the morning bus driver. The evening custodian drove the school bus at the end of the school day. The head custodian, Gary Moore, was a bald man in his late thirties with a thin black mustache. I told him about the panel falling from the ceiling in the first-grade classroom. He put his sandwich on his desk and stood up. "It's a drop ceiling," he said. "Hope no one was hurt. We do things piecemeal around here. When the roof leaked, Les, the former superintendent, sent me up on the roof with a bucket of tar. What are you going to do?" he said. "I'll take care of the ceiling now."

"It fell on an empty desk. No one was hurt." I said.

"Good. The last thing we need is a kid getting hurt," he said. He paused and looked at me. "What am you going to do when the roof leaks?"

"I have no idea, but let's talk about it before the next big rain."

"Yeah. We can talk about it whenever you want," he said walking out of his office and down to the first-grade classroom.

In the spring of that year after a downpour, I called a roofer instead of sending the custodian up with a bucket of tar. What have I gotten myself into? I wondered. Was this board of education in touch with the needs of the school? I knew I would paddle as hard as needed to stay on top of the challenge of being superintendent here, but I realized it was going to be harder, and different, than what I anticipated when I took the job.

On the first day of school, I stood In my brown pin-striped suit in front of the school watching parents drive up in their BMWs and mercedes and drop their kids off. It was a warm and sunny autumn day and I was outside for ten minutes when a black Range Rover pulled up and I saw Michael Jordan behind the wheel. His son, Jeffrey jumped out of the back seat and ran over to join some other kids on the playground. I remembered what Juanita had told me when I ran into her in McDonald's last week, so I strolled over comfortably and introduced myself to Jeffrey's father. I had memorized what I would say to him after Juanita told me he'd be dropping off Jeffrey .

Michael Jordan rolled down his window and I stuck my hand out and said what I'd decided to say. "Hi Michael. My name is Roger Prosise. I'm the superintendent. It's great to have you and your family as a part of our school. If there's anything I can do please let me know."

"Thanks, Captain. I'm pretty sure Jeffrey will do fine but I appreciate it."

We shook hands, I stepped away from the car, and Michael drove off.

That went well, I thought. I stayed outside for ten more minutes before the 8:30 bell rang, amazed that a kid from Cabrini-Green could end up being the superintendent of the school where Michael Jordan's kid went. On the other hand, Michael Jordan himself didn't come from money, so maybe it didn't matter that much. Still, I felt a bit out of place stepping into the role of leader of this school.

After all the kids were inside I stopped in the office to check for messages and discovered that there were no substitute teachers. I still planned to visit classrooms that morning; I always stopped by any new teacher's classroom to see how it was going, I'd been doing that since my first job as a school administrator. But for now I sat at my desk and thought briefly about Cabrini-Green and the day my family moved out of there and into Lake View. Cabrini had good schools—Jenner, although maybe not Cooley, I didn't know much about Bannockburn other than my expectations for it on my first day here. I knew the families were wealthy and the school had very high test scores. The teachers at Jenner, the K through 6th grade school I went to in Cabrini, had high expectations for us and rigorously taught us to think critically. I credit them for making me ready for college. But I was still happy when we moved to Lake View. That move was the biggest change of my life; this change now, from Skokie to Bannockburn, is big but not as big. I made the transition to Lake View and I'll make it here. I found that friends in both places made all the difference and I'm hoping I'll make friends here, though I know I may not as superintendent. It's lonely at the top. Maybe that's what it's like for Michael Jordan too.

I walked down the hall past the blue lockers and stopped in Mr. Riley's classroom to check on the first-year teacher. Twenty students were in the room working on an algebra assignment at their desks. "Everything okay here," I said looking at Mr. Riley, expecting a positive response. He nodded and said, "They're doing an informal algebra assessment." I walked around the room exchanging words with a few of the kids. Some of them liked math more than others, but they were all in their seat and doing their work.

I looked around the room and saw boys and girls dressed in jeans and collared shirts hunched over their desks or talking with the students next to them. I thought about how college was an expectation for these kids, as it was for my own, in contrast to the students I'd encountered in the inner-city schools where I'd worked. Graduation from eighth grade at Tuley, where I had my first regular teaching job, was a special occasion for those kids and their families because the dropout rate for poor inner city high schools was 50 percent. The dropout rate at Cooley was at least 50 percent and probably higher. I had always known I'd go to college. Although my family was poor, my father had a college degree and eventually my older siblings all went to college. But when I was a kid growing up in Cabrini-Green, my expectations about what life would bring me were pretty modest and my view of the world was very limited. I never imagined living anywhere but Cabrini and since my father didn't have a job, I didn't have any career aspirations. I don't remember wanting to be a policeman or fireman or accountant when I was a kid. Role models are critical.

Since my years at Tuley my standard of living and expectations have grown closer to those of the people of Bannockburn and further from the inner city's. I was a home-owner in a well to do suburb, I had a car and college savings plans for my kids. One night in early September, during that first year at Bannockburn, I asked my eighth-grade daughter at dinner about her classes and it became clear to me that the students at her school were expected to go to college. College is not an expectation for poor kids in the inner city, but gangs are, which lead to prison. The high number of students, who drop-out of high school in the inner-city, don't have the skills needed to get a job so they turn to gangs and drug sales. I looked at my daughter and felt grateful for where my life had taken me and therefore her. But I also felt sad for all those poor kids who didn't have a way out.

After ten minutes in Mr. Riley's classroom it was clear to me that all was well and I walked back out into the hall and continued strolling through the school. I passed classrooms with teachers standing at the front writing on chalkboards, teaching classes of twenty students. When I taught at Tuley I had thirty-three kids in my classroom, and that's about what you usually find in Chicago public schools. Here, not only were the classes small but I could see that the students were listening to the teachers and not talking with each other.

After visiting Mr. Riley's classroom, I walked into Ms. Chase's third-grade classroom and sat at an empty desk in the front of the room near the teacher's desk. The daily schedule and classroom rules were posted on the bulletin board next to the door. Four columns of brown student desks and chairs filled the room. The teacher sat in a circle in the back with five students. Students in the circle took turns reading and the teacher threw out questions. A lady in a green short-sleeve shirt and white sweater vest, a teacher aide, sat with a boy at a rectangular table next to the windows and reviewed a page in a workbook. I watched the teachers and kids read, talk, and write for ten minutes and I thought about the benefits of twenty-three kids in the class with a teacher and a teacher aide compared to what happens in a room with thirty-three kids, like the class I had as a teacher at Tuley in the inner city. Class size matters. In small classes teachers have more time to work with individual students.

Money matters, I thought sitting at the front of Ms. Chase's classroom. But then I remembered those teachers and their high expectations and rigorous instruction at Jenner back in 1950s Cabrini and I thought, But it's not everything. The support of a significant adult makes a huge difference in a kid being successful at school.

In the spring when Ms. Chase's third grade class takes the state mandated tests in reading and math, every student will meet or exceed state standards. And in general Bannockburn had really high test scores. They scored consistently as one of the top five schools in the state in reading and math, as determined by the IGAP, the Illinois Goals Assessment Program, which was state's school ranking system at the time. I knew that when I took the job. I remember thinking, I hope the test scores don't drop during my tenure as superintendent there.

I held my first staff meeting on Wednesday of the first week of school. The meeting was in the library at the end of the day. I passed out an agenda to the teachers and gave them a summary of my background as a principal in two previous schools. I remember saying, "I've seen your IGAP scores. I don't know what you're doing, but whatever it is keep it up." The teachers smiled at each other and nodded. There were thirty staff members at the meeting, including teachers and teacher-aides.

In my first year I did a lot of listening and learning. I met with teachers individually and in grade level groups to learn about the needs of the school. Teachers talked about the roof leaking and the need for more classrooms. Based on its high test scores, I decided the curriculum was sound. I attended all of the parent organization meetings during my first year. In all of my previous schools, PTO meetings were held in school libraries, but at Bannockburn the moms took turns hosting them in their homes. At my first PTO meeting I looked around the house and was amazed by how big all the rooms were and how expensive everything seemed. A crystal chandelier hung at the entrance. The kitchen, which was twice the size of the kitchen at my house had cherry cabinets and dark green granite countertops. Even the fish tank, with red, yellow, and blue fish swimming around in it, was huge; it must have held a hundred gallons of water. I felt out of place, but since I was the new superintendent I had to come across as confident. Dressed in a blue suit I had a cup of coffee, met all the moms, and gave a quick report on school activities. I returned to school feeling good about my first PTO meeting at a parent's house. The house was beautiful but I was more comfortable meeting in the school library.

Late on a Friday afternoon, in the winter of my first year at Bannockburn, I stood at the front door of the school watching a cluster of seventh and eighth grade students bundled up in North Face ski coats and caps, load their skis and snowboards into the school bus.

"How many kids are going?" I asked Linda Hampton, the parent who was organizing the ski trip. The kids were going to Wilmot, Wisconsin, about fifty miles away.

"Fifteen," Linda answered. "And we have five chaperones."

"How does that compare to other years?"

"It's about average. We go up for four or five hours and then come back home. We're lucky tonight. There's some snow and you can't complain about the temperature. Do you ski?" Linda asked me.

"I've skied twice but I'm not a skier. Have a great time and be safe," I said.

Once the bus was loaded I got in my car and drove home. Driving down Telegraph Road under a sky full of stars, past the million dollar houses set back on sprawling front lawns covered with snow, I thought about how lucky those kids were.

I remembered how, as the volunteer boys' basketball coach when I was a middle school teacher in the inner-city, we practiced in the school gym and I piled the boys into my van and drove them to the games. That was the only after-school activity for those kids.

As the school year progressed, I got to know the teachers and the parents at Bannockburn. For the most part the parents were happy with the lower school but not with the 7th and 8th grade classes, especially social studies. The parents complained that the social studies teacher, Michele Hines, always taught the same thing every year and the kids were bored in her class. One day in November I went to her classroom when no kids were there and told her about a new social studies program, Facing History and Ourselves, which the neighboring high school was using and which seemed to be popular. The program developed curriculum around major world events like the holocaust and apartheid, for junior high and high school kids. Teachers who used it taught about issues like racism, bigotry, and propaganda, and other social issues. I read brochures about the program and I liked seeing teachers engage kids in conversations about racism and bigotry.

On a cold day in early March, Michelle Hines drove to my house and we carpooled to the two- day conference in down-town Chicago. I participated in the conference as if I was regular teacher. I was impressed by the conversations about race. There was talk about a double standard and African-Americans being treated unfairly by police. We watched a video on the Rodney King beating and talked about the larger implications of the case in terms of race. I remember there were four African-American teachers in the group who were surprised to find so many white people in the group who agreed that there was a double standard and that it was wrong. We also talked about the OJ Simpson case. I thought it would be healthy for kids at Bannockburn to discuss issues of race, even though Bannockburn had a relatively diverse population. Bannockburn was a village of mansions owned mostly by white people, but Trinity International University, a seminary that attracted students from all over the world, was located in Bannockburn, and the graduate students who went there sent their kids to our school. These kids, about twenty percent of the students at Bannockburn School, enriched the environment for everyone. These kids were from countries from all over the world. One year there was a fourth grade girl from Germany. She had blond hair and couldn't speak a word of English.

Sitting in the big classroom at the conference beside Michele, surrounded by fifty other teachers from the city and suburbs of Chicago, I felt proud to be there. I could have just sent Michele to the conference but I didn't. I thought this was a worthwhile program and it should address the parent's concerns about no new lessons in social studies. Michele listened attentively and asked many questions, and when we went back to work she began implementing the program in her classes. When I visited her class, the kids seemed interested in what she was teaching. When she asked questions, three or four students raised their hands and answered the questions. The parents read about the new program in the school newsletter. They liked the new program but they still weren't happy with Michele. Eventually I decided it was really her serious unsmiling affect that they didn't like, not her teaching.

I didn't have any problems with Bannockburn parents until the winter concert in December, the week before Christmas. The day after the concert I got a phone call from a Jewish father who was irate because there were only two Channnukah songs. He yelled and threatened to contact the Anti-Defamation League. Feeling shook up, I hung up the phone. I immediately called the president of the school board, Dennis Levine, who was also Jewish, and told him what had happened.

"Did you have any Channukah songs?" asked Dennis.

"Yeah, we had two."

"Barry expected three. It's people like Barry who give us a bad reputation. You had two songs, don't worry about it."

I appreciated Dennis's support but I still spoke with the music teacher about song selection for the concerts. And when I thought about it I realized the irate parent might have had a point, even though his way of putting it had upset me. At the other schools where I had worked, the holiday season was being celebrated more and more neutrally, with religious songs getting less air time than it used to and neutral songs like Frosty the Snowman getting more play than Christmas carols. But Bannockburn still seemed to take it for granted that the winter holidays were primarily a Christian, Christmas event, with Christmas lights and trees and Santa Claus. I'm a Christian and I celebrate Christmas but in future years to avoid controversy, I told the music teacher to include at least three Channukah songs in the concert.

A shortage of classrooms and the poor condition of the building were the biggest and most immediate needs of the school during my first year there. I recommended a building renovation plan to the board to provide more classrooms. The renovation would cost two million dollars which called for a tax referendum, a property tax increase. The referendum passed overwhelmingly. A successful referendum is evidence of parent support of school. These parents had money and agreed to pay more taxes for their school. I remember when I was a sixth grade student at Jenner School in Cabrini-Green and parents demonstrated support for their school by picketing in front of the school and calling for the principal's resignation.

In my second year and in my third year I oversaw the construction project and it was completed successfully—the old gym was renovated into classrooms and a new gym was added, a computer lab was created in the library and a large school office as well as a new office for me, were also added.

Michael and Juanita Jordan were just like other parents, where moms serve as school volunteers and dads go to special events like concerts and parent/teacher conferences. I remember seeing Michael pushing his youngest son, Marcus, in a swing on the playground as he waited to pick-up Jeffrey from school. In my second year Juanita started volunteering in the office for a couple of hours every Tuesday afternoon, when my secretary had a standing hair appointment. The secretary, Joan, had been at Bannockburn School for more than thirty years and had been taking Tuesdays off to have her hair for most of those years. When I interviewed for my job, a board member referred to Joan as an institution, and once I got the job I decided that her taking Tuesdays off had worked for the other superintendents so I would make it work for me.

Juanita Jordan wanted to be a regular loving mom involved in hers kid's school but she didn't want to be a helicopter parent, as she told one of the teachers, who passed it on to me, so she chose not to volunteer in Jeffrey's classroom. Every Tuesday she showed up dressed casually in jeans or sweatpants and sat at her desk and did her work: answering phones, typing letters, assisting people who came into the office. I found her to be friendly, personable, and down to earth.

Jeffrey Jordan was never more or less than one of the school's 220 students. Michael and Juanita were regular parents who loved their kids, and, like in most families, the mom was more involved in the school than the dad. But they both attended school functions like parent/teacher conferences and curriculum nights and holiday concerts. They even came to the PTO Bingo Night.

In my first year I felt surprised and a little startled when Michael, Juanita, Jeffrey, and Marcus, who was three, walked into the gym filled with families sitting in folding chairs at six-foot tables. I was there walking around, talking with parents, and helped set up chairs as needed. I went over to welcome the Jordans to Bingo Night.

"Is there a table for us?" asked Juanita.

We looked around. All the tables were full except one. The Jordans sat down and all of them, even Marcus, was given a Bingo card. People left them alone and let them play, but every-one was excited they were there. People craned their necks and stared. They stayed the whole night. When they left the gym to go home, a crowd followed, and stood milling around the parking lot until they drove away, although there were no requests for autographs. Afterwards, Brian Banks, the seventh-grade class clown, teased me about shaking Michael's hand when he first came in.

"Tonight was your big night, huh, Dr. Prosise?" he said.

I grinned. "It sure was."

Chapter 22

Diamond Lake

"I want every kid to have a friend," I said.

It was the middle of my first year as superintendent of the Diamond Lake School, a larger more diverse district five miles northwest of Bannockburn. I'd taken the job here because I wanted to work in a school district where I wasn't the only administrator—I was principal and business manager as well as superintendent at Bannockburn, because it was a one-school district with only 220 students—and where there was less diversity among the students.

Diamond Lake District had three schools and all of them had a high percentage of poor Hispanic students. The principals of all three schools, Tanya Johnson, Jodie Hanson, and Chris Watson, were sitting across the table from me today. It was January 7, right after winter break, and we'd been meeting twice a month since September.

The three principals smiled and looked away. "How are we supposed to do that?" asked Chris, the middle school principal.

"What do you think?" I said looking at Tanya and Jodie.

"Most kids have friends," Tanya said.

"But is there any way of knowing if a kid is being left out?" I asked her.

It had come to me as I was cleaning my fish tank last Saturday afternoon that I was lucky to have friends, and that I'd made most of my friends in school. Some of them I'd even known since elementary and high school, like Mike, my first friend after my family moved from Cabrini to Lake View. Mike and I were still hanging out about once a week, going out for breakfast or going to ballgames or neighborhood festivals. Standing there scraping the algae off the sides of my fish tank, I thought of how the parents at my schools often say that their kids can't wait to go back to school at the end of summer to be with their friends. And when you hear about the shooting tragedies in schools, the shooters tend to be loners without friends. Sometimes all you have are friends. And in that moment I made a goal: Every kid at my schools should have at least one friend. I decided to bring it up at the administrative team meeting on Tuesday. I wasn't expecting to make more work for anybody, just to create more awareness on the part of staff.

"What do we do for new students when they transfer in? Are they assigned a buddy?" I said.

"Some teachers ask kids in their class to be buddies with transfer students," Tanya said, "but I don't know if it's across the board. And I think the recess supervisors try to pay attention to whether any kid is being left out, but I'm not really sure how often those kind of problems get addressed."

We went on to the next topic on the agenda, and we wouldn't come back to my goal for another ten years. In the meantime we concentrated on reading and math. Our emphasis at the beginning of my time at Diamond Lake was for every kid to learn how to read or become a better reader. We hired more reading teachers and the new teachers worked with the kids in small groups. My philosophy was that a kid who can read will feel better about herself than a kid who can't read, and a kid who is becoming a better reader will become more confident and better at making friends. We also worked on improving the buildings where it all the learning took place—we needed more classrooms and held a district-wide referendum. The taxpayers voted to approve a small tax increase and we used the money to double the size of the middle school, add 7500-square feet to the grammar school, and renovate the primary school. All of that took about five years. Our reading and math scores continued to get better year after year, and one day, after I had been at Diamond Lake for about ten years, it came to me that we had accomplished most of the goals we'd had when I started out in the district. Maybe it was was time to move on to another goal, I thought. And then I remembered my goal of every kid having a friend.

Driving home at the end of the day, I decided to learn more about what other schools were doing to help their kids socialize. At work the next morning I picked up the phone and called someone at a program I knew of at the University of Illinois-Chicago: CASEL (Collaborative of Academic, Social and Emotional Learning), which had been started by Tim Shriver and Roger Weissburg in 1994 and became the nation's leading organization advancing the development of academic and social, and emotional competence for students. And two months later, two Diamond Lake principals, a board member, and I attended a two-day CASEL conference. At the conference we learned about various school programs that help kids make friends and develop emotionally, and at work the following Monday I set up a new meeting to discuss what we'd learned. At that meeting I told a committee of teachers and parents about the programs discussed at the CASEL conference. One of the programs that really interested me, Responsive Classroom, involved twenty-minute meetings at the beginning of class every day where the kids had a chance to talk about personal concerns with the teacher and each other. As soon as I told the teachers and parents at our meeting about it, two of the teachers said they'd used it when they worked at other schools and it helped kids solve problems without fighting and open up and make friends. That sold it for everybody.

That summer twenty-five Diamond Lake teachers went to a one-week training session in Wisconsin, and in the fall, in every classroom in the Diamond Lake School District, kids started opening up to each other and talking more freely than they usually did, in class meetings.

"How was the bus ride to school this morning?" Mrs. Wilson asked her third-grade class at a class meeting one morning in October. She was sitting in a chair in the middle of a circle of kids sitting on the floor around her. I was seated at a student desk observing, trying not to interfere or attract attention. The students went around clockwise. Nobody had much to say. Mostly they just nodded and said, "It was okay." Then we came to James, a small boy with blond hair. "When I was on the bus yesterday some older kids wouldn't let me sit in a seat," he said in a clear piping voice. "I told them I would scream if they didn't let me sit down."

"Do you know who they are?" I said.

Two kids in the circle nodded knowingly and looked sympathetically at James. One of them, a tall girl named Elizabeth, said, "I know their names."

"Good. Give them to me," Mrs. Wilson said. "Thank you, Elizabeth. Now let's talk about what happened to James on the bus yesterday. How did you feel when it happened, James?"

James told the class that the bullies let him sit down on the bus but they looked mad and he was afraid and he was scared to come to school today. When he finished talking he looked around the room at the other kids sitting. The boy next to him put his arm around his shoulders and everybody else smiled and nodded encouragingly. "I'll save you a seat on the bus this afternoon," one boy said. James smiled more broadly.

I was glad James was feeling better, happy that a program I'd help implement was making him and the other kids in this school open up and feel safer. And then it occurred to me that in the suburbs kids have to worry about getting bullied on the bus and in the inner city kids have worry about getting shot at while walking home. Both groups of kids are at risk and need help. I wondered if there was any way I could do something for the kids being shot at on their way home from school.

But for now I was here in the Diamond Lake District. In the end I would stay here for another four years, fourteen years in all. The Responsive Classroom Program helped many kids with all kinds of problems—feeling left out, being picked on the playground, having their best friend move away. It helped kids develop emotional intelligence, another one of our goals after

I became superintendent at Diamond Lake. And it went a long way toward helping many kids have more friends. But I thought we could still do more.

I walked around the gym talking with teachers and watching students fill brown cardboard boxes with cereal, pasta, canned corn, and other food. It was 2010; I'd been superintendent at Diamond Lake for twelve years. This year we had a new program in the middle school, Rachel's Challenge. The program was named after Rachel Scott, who was the first student killed in the shooting at Columbine High School in 1999. After the shooting Rachel's father started Rachel's Challenge, a program with the goal of replacing violence and bullying in school with acts of kindness and respect, as practiced and desired by his daughter Rachel.

West Oak, the middle school in Diamond Lake, formed a Rachel's Challenge committee and the committee decided a food drive would be a good place to start. The kids made flyers and posters and there was an article in the school newsletter, and parents and other people in the community brought non-perishable food to the school and left it in boxes in the lobby. posters And this afternoon the middle-school students and a couple of teachers were packing the food up for the homeless shelter. I was in the audience during the Rachel's Challenge kick-off assembly a year ago and I've been looking forward to seeing it enacted ever since.

I walked over to the table where Mrs. Wilson, the reading teacher, was standing. Three girls walked by and picked up some Cheerios and Wheaties to take to the table with all the cereal. "Nice job, girls," I said as they walked past me.

They giggled and smiled.

"Earlier in the year, one of my seventh graders, Natalie Gomez, was in the homeless shelter where this is going," said Mrs. Wilson.

"How'd she get out?"

"She moved in with her grandma. There she is now laughing with the other girls." Mrs. Wilson pointed to a tall dark-haired girl wearing a green dress. She was industriously packing cans of corn into a box and talking happily to a group of four other girls.

"How's she doing?"

"She needs extra support with reading but she's making friends. She journaled about the shelter in my class. I wouldn't want to live there. No privacy at all."

"That's a great story," I said, thinking about how I had been poor but never homeless. I looked at Natalie again. She looked happy and healthy and surrounded by friends. Rachel's Challenge hadn't helped her get out of the homeless shelter and into a home with her grandmother, but I could see how doing things like this—participating in a community service project with her friends, inspired by Rachel's Challenge, helping others—was helping her thrive. And it was also helping her make more friends.

I walked away from the table feeling happy, happy in my life and in my job, happy for Natalie Gomez and all the other kids whose lives I got to witness and try to make a difference in.

It was the end of my time in Diamond Lake and I looked forward to the change, but would miss the people.

"B-52," Tanya yelled from the stage in the gym at West Oak School.

I put a red plastic token on my card. I was sitting at a table with Sharon Taylor, the PTO president, Colette Altman, Diamond Lake's business manager, and John Ward, the band teacher. It was May 12, a few weeks away from the end of my last year at Diamond Lake. I had been a superintendent for eighteen years and I wanted to explore other options, like consulting and writing. It was time for something new. I also had my eye on becoming the principal of Jenner, the elementary school I went to in Cabrini-Green so many years ago, although as it would turn out I would only end up volunteering there. Chicago was closing its inner-city schools by then, and although they never closed Jenner, they weren't hiring a new principal for it.

I was two squares away from Bingo. This was the third annual PTO family bingo night. The gym was filled with families sitting at round tables, and food and drinks were for sale on the far side of the gym. I noticed that Alejandra Rodriquez was playing bingo with her parents and her little brother Edwardo at the table next to mine. I'd known Alejandra a little since she was in third grade, in the same way I knew most of the other students at Diamond Lake, but I didn't learn that she was an artist till the principal of West Oak said at a board meeting that her paintings were on display for sale at the Cultural Center in North Chicago. I couldn't make it to the show, but Alejandra's mother let me look at Alejandra's work in the basement of their house and after that I commissioned Alejandra to do a painting of Diamond Lake—the actual lake, which attracted summer vacationers—and hung it in my office.

A person yelled "Bingo!" across the room, and I stood up and stretched my legs, then walked to Alejandra's table. Marisol Ortiz, a student I knew had moved from Mexico to the area at the beginning of the school, was sitting next to Alejandra. I sat down for a brief chat. "How do you like West Oak?" I asked Marisol.

"Everyone has been friendly, especially Alejandra."

Alejandra and I looked at each other and smiled. "I was her buddy last fall," said Alejandra. I nodded. At the beginning of the school year the West Oak teachers had accepted Rachel's Challenge and started a new buddy system in their classes.

"Tell me about being a buddy," I said to both of them.

"I looked out for her and helped her with school," Alejandra said.

"She introduced me to her friends," Marisol said, smiling shyly. "Now I know lots of kids."

I smiled broadly and stood up. We had accomplished my goal. It wasn't really my goal; it was a goal that belonged the whole school, the whole district. And there was probably more to be done. There was always more to be done. But we were making good progress. Every kid, or at least many kids, maybe most of our kids at Diamond Lake, had a friend.

Chapter 23
Fish Sticks and Corn on the Cob

I'm sitting at a table in the back of the room with three sixth-grade boys, waiting for the teacher to begin the lesson on prayer. Another volunteer, Tom, a young man from Moody Bible Institute who volunteers at By the Hand every day, is sitting with us. We're in a classroom in the Lower North Center, a small concrete-block community center owned by the Chicago Park District, in what used to be called Cabrini-Green. I'm volunteering in an after-school program called By the Hand. By the Hand is a non-profit Christian organization that helps kids in distressed circumstances grow academically and spiritually.

I retired from Diamond Lake four years ago, and since the door to becoming a principal of an inner city school never opened, I've decided to find other ways to help poor kids succeed in school. I learned about the opportunity to volunteer in Cabrini-Green from a friend one day at church. I thought it would be worthwhile to go back to my old neighborhood and connect to my roots. Mostly though, I wanted to give back some of what I had been given. I knew school helped me get out of poverty and I wanted to be part of helping other kids get out of poverty in any way I could.

There are fifteen sixth-graders, a teacher and a teacher aid, and five volunteers in the room. The kids have already eaten downstairs in the gym with the whole group, about eighty kids in first through eighth grades, all of them poor, all of them African-American. Every day they get a meal before the tutoring starts. The Lower North Center is next to the Jenner School, where I went for kindergarten through sixth grade. Kids from Jenner walk here after school for the By the Hand after-school programs, and kids from three other inner-city elementary schools arrive by bus every afternoon between three-thirty and four. When my family lived in Cabrini-Green my brothers and sisters and I went to the Lower North Center for after-school activities and now here I am fifty years later, about to start tutoring kids at the same place.

The Lower North Center is in a different building now from the one I was in, and Jenner is also in a different building. The building I went to school in was torn down years ago and replaced by condos. What used to be the Cabrini neighborhood is called River North and is largely made up of fifteen-story glass and silver high rises inhabited by mostly white people with money, but the rowhouses are still here, standing there on prime property while the city of Chicago figures out what to do with them. Most of them are vacant, but about 150 families still live there in public housing. The kids from the rowhouses go to Jenner School, just like I did.

The teacher starts the short Bible study class. He reads Philippians 4:6 from the Bible and then asks the kids, "What should we do instead of worrying?" Rodney Jones, a boisterous sixth-grader sitting at the table next to me—Rodney goes to Jenner School like I did—raises his hand and shouts, "Pray to God."

"That's right. Leave things in God's hands," Mr. Marcus says firmly. Twenty minutes later, after reading more Bible verses and discussing them with the kids, Mr. Marcus closes his Bible and says it's time for tutoring and I turn to Serenity, Rodney, and Chris, while Tom, the other volunteer, looks on.

I tell them my name and that I went to Jenner School just like they do and that I lived in the rowhouses when I was their age. The three of them stare at me unblinkingly. I wait for a reaction and am surprised when there isn't one. No questions about when I moved or what Cabrini was like when I lived there. I don't know what I expected them to say or do but I expected something. Maybe living in Cabrini isn't a big deal to them, I think, and then decide that makes sense: Why would it be? It wasn't a big deal to me either when I lived there and it was only later, when everybody acted like it was strange that I had grown up there, that I started thinking there was something out of the ordinary about my experience. I ask Serenity, Rodney, and Chris about their families, wondering if I might know any of their grandparents. Rodney says he has an older sister who's a freshman in college at UIC.

I'm surprised. "That's great. Are you thinking of going to college?" I ask him, even though he's only in sixth grade.

He nods. I feel encouraged and wonder how I can help him. The Posse Foundation crosses my mind. Posse is a national organization that partners with colleges and universities to provide full scholarships to promising high school students from urban backgrounds, young people who are not the typical college-bound student. Every year, in Chicago, approximately twelve hundred students apply for eighty Posse slots. The students who are selected are assigned to colleges in groups of ten, or 'posses.' Nine years ago I tutored three high school seniors who were starting college in the fall, getting full four-year scholarships due to the Posse Foundation. Maybe Rodney can be as lucky as they were, I think hopefully.

Now it's four o'clock on Thursday afternoon and I'm in the third week of volunteering in the Lower North Center. I'm wearing clear rubber gloves and standing behind a table filled with eight pans of fish sticks and corn on the cob, doing the other part of my job. The kids eat first, then go upstairs to be tutored. All eighty of them are lined up holding trays with plates and silverware. They process through the line and I put fish sticks and corn on their plates. Rodney comes back for seconds after everyone has been through the line once.

"Could I have some more?" Rodney asks holding out his tray.

I scoop up two more fish sticks and put them on his plate. The smell of frying fish reminds me of eating in the mess hall in my church summer camp, Camp Lake Chi Ko.

Rodney smiles broadly, thanks me, and returns to his table on the far side of the gym. I throw away my rubber gloves and join him and some of the other sixth graders at a long table by the windows. After all the kids are finished eating, everyone in the cafeteria goes upstairs to the classrooms. I follow the sixth graders to Room 211 at the end of the hall. The kids I'm tutoring today, Serenity, Taj, and Daryl, find a round table in the corner of the room and sit down. I join them and so does Bob, one of the other volunteers. Serenity opens her backpack and pulls out a stack of papers and a notebook, getting ready to work on her math homework.

"I got a B on my test," she says with a large smile.

"You did. Wow. Congratulations."

"Thank you for helping me."

I work with different kids every week, but it so happens I've had Serenity in my group for all three weeks I've been coming here. I don't enjoy driving in traffic for an hour to get to Cabrini-Green, but I do like working with the kids. Serenity always has homework and she always wants to learn and do well in school. Last week she told me she might have to stop coming to this after-school program because she might move to the southside to live with her mother. Right now she's living with her grandma on the near northside. I worry about how moving would affect her progress in school. She's happy about the prospect of living with her mother but she still wants to go to By the Hand and she won't be able to if she moves.

Even though dishing out fish sticks and corn on the cob to eighty poor black kids isn't the most challenging project I've undertaken, feeding and helping these kids with their homework makes me feel like I'm making a difference.

I look at Serenity, Taj, and Daryl and a wave of affectionate nostalgia comes over me. I wonder how much they know about life outside of Cabrini, whether they're even interested in living outside Cabrini. I remember how I turned down a scholarship to Illinois Wesleyan, partly because I couldn't imagine going away somewhere to college. I open the math workbook in front of me and start helping Serenity with a long division problem while Tom works with Taj and Daryl.

Endnotes

Petty, Audrey. High Rise Stories: Voices from Chicago Public Housing, 2013

Austen, Ben. "The last tower: the decline and fall of public housing," Harper's Magazine, May 2012

Wilkerson, Isabel, The Warmth of Other Suns, 2010

Reeves, Richard. Infamy: the shocking story of the Japanese American internment of World War II.

Shiozaki, Cory. The Manzanar Fishing Club film

The Chicago Schools: A Social and Political History; Mary Herrick, 1970

Places of Their Own: African American Suburbanization in the Twentieth Century, Andrew Wiese

"The Last Tower," Harper's Magazine, (Ben Austen) May 2012

High Rise Stories: Voices from Chicago Public Housing Voice of Witness (Audrey Petty)

Housing Projects, Mansions and Schools:

Biography

Roger Prosise was a school administrator in the suburbs of Chicago for over twenty-five years. He started his career as a teacher in the inner city of Chicago. He has a Ph.D. from Loyola University Chicago. He is an associate with the Ray and Associates Search Firm. He is married to Ellen and has three adult children, two of whom are married, Lauren/Andrew Kimura, Kristen/Dan Guzzardo, and Kevin Prosise. He also has three grandkids, Madeline, Lily, and Claire.

65496438R00088

Made in the USA
Lexington, KY
14 July 2017